The Royal Mile and New Town

Lang**Syne**

PUBLISHING

WRITING *to* REMEMBER

Publisher's note

Our cover shows Princes Street in 1825, and the start of the building of the Royal Institution, painted by Alexander Naysmith. Reproduced by kind permission of the National Galleries of Scotland.
Content in *The Vanished Mile* chapter had been edited and condensed from Robert T. Skinner's *The Royal Mile*, published in 1947 by Oliver and Boyd. The engravings are reproduced from *Old and New Edinburgh* by James Grant, published in 1882 by Cassell, Petter, Galpin and Co.

Frontispiece: Edinburgh Castle, as it was before the siege of 1573.

Lang**Syne**

PUBLISHING

WRITING *to* REMEMBER

Strathclyde Business Centre
120 Carstairs Street, Glasgow G40 4JD
Tel: 0141 554 9944 Fax: 0141 554 9955
E-mail: scottish-memories.co.uk

Printed by Dave Barr Print, Glasgow
Design and artwork by Roy Boyd and David Braysher
© Lang Syne Publishers Ltd 2003
ISBN 0-946264-92-9

The Royal Mile and New Town

PROSPECT OF EDINBURGH, FROM THE NORTH, 1693. *(After Slezer.)*

PROSPECT OF EDINBURGH CASTLE, FROM THE NORTH, 1779.
(After an engraving in Hugo Arnot's "History of Edinburgh.")

THE OLD TOWN, FROM PRINCES STREET.
(From an engraving by J. Clark of a painting by A. Kay, 1814.)

THE CASTLE, RAMSAY GARDENS, BANK OF SCOTLAND, AND EARTHEN
MOUND, FROM PRINCES STREET. *(From an engraving by J. Clark, 1814.)*

NEW YEAR'S EVE AT THE TRON CHURCH, IN THE 1880s.

EDINBURGH, FROM MONS MEG BATTERY, 1880.

THE REGISTER HOUSE, 1880. *(From a photograph by G.W. Wilson & Co., Aberdeen.)*

HERIOT'S HOSPITAL, FROM THE SOUTH-WEST, 1880.

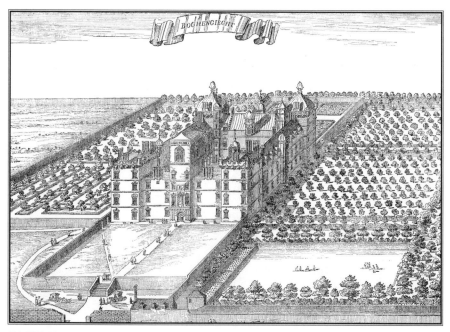

FACSIMILE OF AN OLD ENGRAVING OF HERIOT'S HOSPITAL. *(After Slezer.)*

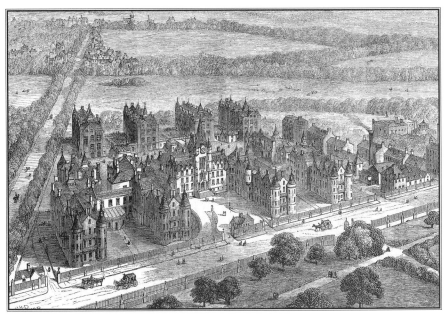

BIRD'S-EYE VIEW OF THE ROYAL INFIRMARY, FROM THE NORTH-EAST, 1878.

THE FORMER GENERAL POST OFFICE, 1882.

HERIOT'S HOSPITAL. *1. The Hospital, 1779; 2. Porter's Lounge; 3. Dining Hall; 4. Quadrangle, looking north; 5. Quadrangle, looking south.*

THE HIGH SCHOOL, ERECTED IN 1578.

THE SECOND HIGH SCHOOL, 1820. *(After Storer).*

THE INDUSTRIAL MUSEUM, 1880.
1. Exterior; 2. The Great Hall; 3. The Natural History Room.

THE TEMPLE LANDS, GRASSMARKET, 1850s. *(From a drawing by George Simson.)*

OLD HOUSES, 1852. *(From a drawing by George W. Simson.)*

1. HERIOT ROW; 2. ROYAL CIRCUS; 3. INDIA PLACE; 4. AINSLIE PLACE;
5. MORAY PLACE, 1885.

GEORGE WATSON'S HOSPITAL, 1819.

EDINBURGH CASTLE FROM PORT HOPETOUN, 1825. *(After Ewbank.)*

contents

Introduction

The Royal Mile, Scotland's most historic thoroughfare, and the New Town, with its magnificent Georgian architecture, give Edinburgh a unique character.

The tenements, wynds and closes of the High Street are in sharp contrast to the elegantly planned squares and crescents of the more modern town which dates from the eighteenth century.

In ancient times Edinburgh began as a fortress on top of an extinct volcano and a few primitive dwellings. Today that volcano is dominated by Edinburgh Castle and from here it is a mile to the Palace of Holyroodhouse which serves as the Queen's official residence during her visits to Edinburgh.

CASTLEHILL, 1845.

This Royal Mile is divided into different sections: Castlehill, Lawnmarket, High Street, and Canongate. With the passing of the centuries a fascinating story has unfolded and in the following pages you can find out about the people, places and events which have helped shape its character.

Many of the stories featured are unusual and include: the riddle of the fish hawker who came back to life after being hanged; the spooky soldiers of the castle; the witch who sank ships; the lover ruined by tulips; the close haunted by headless ghosts; and the murderers who sold their victims' bodies to doctors for research.

The stories of Holyrood and St Giles tell why an Edinburgh mob ripped open the coffins in a Royal Vault and scattered bones everywhere, how a cancelled wedding led to the destruction of the Palace and the Abbey, how a miracle followed a King's encounter with a deadly stag, why a Royal supper party ended in cold blooded murder, who was a Royal bride at 12 and why the Cathedral was once destroyed.

When, in 1766, the Royal Mile and the surrounding area had become overcrowed plans were invited for the design of a New Town. It was a pioneering bold attempt at civic planning and spawned what is today one of the largest unspoiled classical romantic developments in Europe.

Although a mere youngster when set against the Old Town there are many strange stories to be explored here. Those featured include: the witches who were 'tried' in Princes Street Gardens and burned alive at Picardy Place; the opium poisoner of George Street; New Town ghosts such as Merry Jack Tar the naughty sailor; the affairs of a Rose Street woman who scandalised her neighbours and had to be hounded out of town; the antics of a key forger, from the same place, who wrecked the peace of Princes Street Gardens; the facts behind local murders; and the 'stolen' afternoon at the races which led to the birth of a great department store.

You can find out, too, about the villages, hamlets and highways that ran through the area before planners had even dreamed of a New Town and the extraordinary steps taken to get people to live and work here after the plans were approved by our eighteenth century administrators.

There is a full guide to places of interest in both the Royal Mile and New Town and 20 facts about "Modern Athens".

VIEW OF THE CASTLE & CITY OF EDINBURGH.
(Reduced facsimile of a print published in 1575.)

Haunted!

The Royal Mile probably has more ghost stories linked to it than any other thoroughfare in Britain. Hardly surprising when one considers that it has seen hundreds of violent deaths caused by murder, disease and suicide down through history.

Some of the yarns were invented by our ancestors during ale-drinking sessions in local taverns, but others - like the spooks of Mary King's Close - are too horrific for man alone to invent. It was disease that created them.

Today the close remains sixty feet below the City Chambers in a remarkable state of preservation - four centuries after the Great Plague wiped out most of its inhabitants.

More people died there per square yard than anywhere else in Edinburgh. As the death toll began to mount, city magistrates stepped in and ordered the close to be sealed off so that the disease "would be prevented from spreading". For many years the houses stood empty, but as time passed demand for accommodation in the overcrowded capital grew. And one day a few homeless families, ignoring local superstitions, decided to move into a crumbling tenement in the Close.

But they weren't there for long. Ghosts of people and animals who had died of the plague appeared and frightened them out of their wits.

A Mr and Mrs Thomas Coltheart were first to see the spirits. A few days earlier they had laughingly dismissed a warning from an old fortune teller who said: "You will have company there other than yourself."

While sitting reading the Bible on their first Sunday afternoon in the house the candlelight suddenly turned blue. Then a head appeared, suspended in mid-air. A few minutes later a naked arm turned up holding a lamp, followed by ghostly dancing feet! The strange gathering was completed by the arrival of a headless dog and cat. Similar events happened in other homes.

Needless to say the frightened families immediately packed their belongings and fled. Once again the Close fell into decay - this time for good. A fire in 1750 reduced many of the weed covered tenements to ruin and three years later the remainder was incorporated in the west side of the Royal Exchange. This fine building was originally a centre where the merchants of Edinburgh could conduct their business in comfort away from the overcrowded, foul-smelling High Street.

There are regular, organised tours of the Close, which is still visible from Cockburn Street. Despite a modern network of wires, pipes and tubes, a recognisable lane can be seen rising to the High Street. Massive vaulted chambers lead off it. The ancient wooden doorways are still there and hooks

THE ROYAL EXCHANGE, IN THE 1860s.

remain embedded in the ceiling of what was probably a butcher's shop. Today Mary King is just a memory, but it's not difficult to see why many of our ancestors ended up wishing they'd never heard the name.

Meanwhile we return to the surface again... and climb aboard the "Death Coach". Sightings of this ghostly wagon are recorded in several old documents. It's supposed to appear before a disaster and gallop from Holyrood to the castle drawn by headless horses emitting "flashes of fire".

If during your journey down the Royal Mile you hear the strains of pipe music coming from beneath the ground, don't be too surprised.

In the early years of the nineteenth century a tunnel is supposed to have been discovered running from a castle dungeon to the Palace. A young piper agreed to explore it. He was told to keep playing so that the crowd above could follow. But halfway down the music stopped and the man was never seen again.

The Castle is naturally the scene of many spooky tales. In the reign of King Charles II a squadron of ghost troops gave two sentries the shock of their lives. They were part of a detachment of soldiers garrisoned there under the command of Colonel Dundas to counter a threatened attack from Cromwell's army. Just after midnight on his first watch the sentry heard the sound of drums beating out an old Scots march and the trudge of many feet in the distance. He immediately fired his musket and Dundas rushed to the spot. But there was nobody there. Dundas, furious, had the baffled sentry locked up.

Less than an hour had passed when his replacement had a similar experience. This time Dundas decided to take over the watch himself and he, too, heard the drums and tramping of feet. Some say that the ghostly troops can still be heard to this day at a few minutes past midnight!

Men and women murdered at the Castle rank amongst the most frequent visitors. They include the steward of a former Governor, the Duke of Gordon. He was stabbed to death by Gordon in 1689 after the boat, in which he was taking his master's wife and children to Fife, sank during a storm in the Forth. There are a number of accounts written by people who say they've seen the troubled spirit of the steward on the anniversary of his murder. One of the most vivid was by Robert Eliot Westwood, an instructor in the Royal Engineers, who saw it when living in part of the Governor's House in the 1880s.

Once the Castle was a hold for Jacobite prisoners, among them Lord Balcarres. On the night of July 27,1689, Balcarres got a shock when he drew aside the curtains of his bed to retire for the evening. For lying staring at him was Graham of Claverhouse, Viscount Dundee. Balcarres spoke to his friend but didn't receive a reply. This was hardly surprising - at that very hour the viscount was lying dead at Kiliecrankie. Again, it's said, Dundee's ghost has been seen many times on the anniversary of this battle.

On the night before the Battle of Flodden, ghostly heralds appeared at the Cross of Edinburgh and called out the names of those who would die in the forthcoming battle. Richard Lawson, a well-known city gentleman of the day, was walking up the deserted High Street when he heard the chilling announcement. The sky turned scarlet as the death list, which began with the King's name, was read out. Lawson was horrified when he heard the twelfth name - it was his own. He dropped to his knees and said a prayer. Obviously it was answered. He was the only man mentioned in the list who returned from the bloody battle.

It is difficult to establish the veracity of this story. Some historians say that the incident was probably staged by Margaret Tudor to prevent her husband marching to England.

For our next tale in this Royal Mile ghost tour we travel down to Canongate, once an independent burgh where rich and poor lived side by side in the same closes. One of its better-known ghost stories concerns a girl who appeared during a fire which broke out in a house standing near the top of the Canongate. The daughter of a wealthy influential family, she brought shame on them when it was discovered she was expecting the child of a servant. The pregnancy was kept secret and the girl forbidden to leave the

THE MARQUIS OF HUNTLY'S
HOUSE, FROM THE CANONGATE.

house. When the baby was born a minister was called, and instructed to perform the Last Rites. He had been told on arriving at the house that the girl was dying, yet she appeared to be in reasonable enough health. His suspicion deepened when he heard the cry of a newborn baby from the next room. But when the minister started to ask questions he was told to keep quiet if he valued his life. A purse full of gold coins was thrust into his hands by the girl's father as he left.

The baffled minister carried on with the rest of his calls. When he returned to the manse later he learned that a house had been burned down in the Canongate and a young lady killed. A check on the address revealed that it was the one he had visited earlier. However he was frightened of what the family might do if he spoke out and it was only before his own death, many years later, that the minister finally broke his silence.

Meantime the house had been rebuilt but in the middle of the eighteenth century it again caught fire. A young woman dressed in clothes belonging to the early seventeenth century stood amidst the flames crying: "Once burned, twice burned, the third time I'll scare you all".

Satan's Invisible World Discovered, a quaint old book which must have sent many chills down the spines of our great great grannies, contains several unusual ghost stories. One concerned an amorous butcher who found a girlfriend in Provost's Close, only four days after the funeral of his late wife. While in the arms of his new lover the butcher looked up at the window - and saw the sad, cold face of his wife, her grave clothes flowing in the wind. He was frightened but, despite the eerie incident, went back to the house a few days later. The same thing happened again. Shortly afterwards, the butcher caught a disease from which he never recovered.

THE NETHERBOW PORT,
FROM THE CANONGATE.

THE PALACE GATE. *(After an etching by James Skene of Rubislaw.)*

THE CANONGATE, LOOKING WEST.
(From a drawing by Shepherd, published in 1829.)

Back from the dead!

In the early part of the eighteenth century, a sensation was caused in Edinburgh over the case of High Street fish hawker, Margaret Dickson. For she came back to life after being hanged!

The story began in 1723 when Maggie's husband deserted her shortly after the birth of their second son. Brokenhearted, she decided to pay a visit to relatives in Newcastle to take her mind off things.

En route, Maggie stopped for the night at an inn in the quiet Borders town of Kelso. She liked the landlady and decided to stay on for a while, helping around the place in return for free board and lodgings.

Maggie's happy-go-lucky life there turned sour when she discovered that she was pregnant to William Bell, the owner's son. Her attempts to conceal the pregnancy resulted in the child being born prematurely and after only a few days he died.

Maggie decided to throw the body into the River Tweed but lost her nerve when she reached the bank. Instead she hid it in some long grass near the water's edge.

EAST END OF THE GRASSMARKET, SHOWING THE WEST BOW, THE GALLOWS, AND OLD CORN MARKET. *(Facsimile of an etching by James Skene of Rubislaw.)*

A few hours later a fisherman discovered the baby and immediately notified the local magistrates. Maggie was eventually traced. She was charged under the Concealment of Pregnancy Act of 1690 and returned to Edinburgh for trial. The court found the young fisherwoman guilty and imposed a sentence of death by hanging.

Maggie was a very popular local character and the crowd which turned up for her execution in the Grassmarket on September 2, 1724, numbered several thousands. Some friends brought a cart and coffin so that they could give her a decent burial. As the body was cut down by the hang-man they got involved in a scuffle with a number of medical students who were determined to get it for dissecting at Surgeon's Hall. The crowd was outraged and gave the unfortunate medics a sound thrashing!

Later that afternoon the life of fun-loving Maggie was recalled in local taverns. Meanwhile, a few miles away, Maggie's friends heard groans coming from inside the coffin as they turned into the graveyard at Musselburgh. They opened the lid and were astonished to discover that she was alive!

For a few weeks Maggie was very weak but eventually made a full recovery. The question now being asked was: "Will she be tried again?" Top legal brains of the day considered the case but their verdict was that Maggie would have to go free as she had already been pronounced dead by the magistrates. She lived for another 40 years — carrying the nickname "Half Hangit Maggie Dickson" everywhere she went.

THE LAWNMARKET, FROM THE SITE OF THE WEIGH-HOUSE, 1825.

During the latter half of these 40 years Edinburgh was falling increasingly into the grip of General Joe Smith, a hunchbacked little cobbler who lived in a Canongate tenement. He was a sort of Robin Hood - robbing the rich to give to the poor.

The magistrates were frightened to death of General Joe and he virtually ran the city, always taking care not to go too far and antagonise Government authorities. His long unkempt hair and piercing eyes made him look vicious, which he could easily be if some poor person got a raw deal.

At a moment's notice the General could summon a huge army of citizens simply by walking down the High Street beating a drum. At one point, it's said, Joe's following numbered 10,000. Peasants flooded out of closes and vennels like rats following the Pied Piper of Hamelin.

One day a crowd of Joe's followers beat a wealthy city landlord to death and burned his home to the ground. The reason? A few hours earlier, the man had evicted a family called Gordon from their home in the Pleasance for falling into arrears with rent. Seeing his wife and children in tears, Mr Gordon hanged himself.

A few years later, at a time of poverty and near famine, Joe ordered grain dealers to slash the price of their goods. One, however, slyly reduced his measures by one quarter - and proudly boasted about what he had done to some friends. Joe heard about this and ordered the dealer to pay back a quarter of what he had charged each customer. Next day he raised a crowd to ransack the cheat's shop.

Many similar actions to these made General Joe Smith the hero of Edinburgh's poor and underprivileged citizens. So it's not surprising to find that thousands attended his funeral in 1780. He was killed in a fall from a stagecoach while drunk.

Another worthy of the day, who also adopted a title he didn't deserve, was Daft Bailie Jamie Duff. As a child, Jamie always stood out because of his bedraggled appearance. And in his late teens he surprised everyone by starting to dress like a bailie. From the day of his 19th birthday to the day he died, Jamie strutted around the streets wearing a brass chain around his neck and a cocked hat and wig on his head.

Every morning the mock magistrate visited kirkyards to ask the sextons if any funerals were planned for that day and if so when they would take place. He would always walk in front of the mourners with his hat in his hands.

On one occasion, Jamie was collecting water from a well near his mother's home in the Canongate when he spotted a funeral procession approaching. With buckets still in hand he joined in, little realising that the procession was heading for South Queensferry on the shores of the Firth of Forth! Once there, the mourners took a boat across the Firth for the burial in

THE CANONGATE TOLBOOTH, 1880.

Fife. Jamie couldn't understand what was happening and, already weary with walking, began the long journey back home. When he finally reached the Canongate some five hours later, Jamie was heard to mutter that he had never been at "sic a daft like burial before, for there was nae grave at it".

Edinburgh was a particularly romantic place in those far-off days and had more than its fair share of wooers.

One of the better-known, but less fortunate ones, was Captain Hay - nicknamed the Daft Captain. He would march around, head held high, expecting every young lady who passed by to fall madly in love with him.

Unfortunately he was half blind and had an unfortunate habit of walking right up to women and peering at them. This amused many members of the gentler sex who, on seeing Jamie approach, would pull their veils over their heads. Eventually Jamie hit back by getting a veil himself and a placard which read:

"I know what you mean,
I'm too ugly to be seen".

Sadly, the Daft Captain never did find his true love and died a bachelor in 1804.

Alexander Thomson, a wealthy businessman who had a grocer's shop opposite the Tron Kirk, was another one who didn't have much success. He was known locally as the Prince of Grocers. Alexander decided that his bride would have to be a member of the aristocracy but they didn't approve. Of the dozens of wealthy ladies he tried to win favour with, not one was interested.

James Justice, a principal clerk in the Court of Session, was convinced that "saying it with tulips" was the best way to a maiden's heart. And the more unusual the tulip the better. He would not hesitate to pay £50 or more for a single rare root. Eventually James was forced to sell his estate to pay off tulip bills!

In the nineteenth century one of the Royal Mile's best-known preachers was a man who never once spoke from a church pulpit. He was Daddy Flockhart, whose eccentricities and pawky sayings eventually became known around the world. Daddy, a native of Glasgow, was converted to Christianity by an army sergeant while serving in India. He preached from a chair at the railing of St Giles, always praying with his eyes open. Daddy did this because one evening, shortly after he'd started his career as an unofficial clergyman, a prostitute ran off with the collection box while the Lord's Prayer was being recited.

Among his best-known phrases were: "I wad like to load Mons Meg wi' Bibles and fire salvation doon the Canongate", and "When Ah'm fleein' up tae Heaven efter deein' the rowdy women o' the High Street'll try and haud on tae ma coat so Ah will mak sure tae wear a jackit that day". Daddy died in 1857.

Feed the Ravens was a popular street seller who had stances in the Lawnmarket and Canongate. He was full of patter and did an excellent trade hawking gingerbread. Before selling he would throw pieces of cake to his audience and shout: "Feed the Ravens! Feed the Ravens!"

Cocoanut Tam, real name Thomas Simpson, was another famous worthy. He was a hunchback and used to conduct his trade from outside the Tron Kirk crying all the time: "Cocoanit! Cocoanit! A ha'penny the bit". Tam was born in Strichen's Close, High Street, and died in Potterrow aged 71.

There were, of course, many other interesting characters down through the centuries who helped make the Royal Mile such a fascinating place. But to name them would take at least a dozen volumes.

Not all lived there on a permanent basis. Some came into the city from the surrounding towns and villages to do business. Others spent the weekends having a good time in the taverns. For the Royal Mile, with its romantic and exciting lifestyle, was a favourite spot where folk could pursue the shadier activities of life without being spotted by the neighbours.

However, in the mid-fifteenth century magistrates, who had enough on their hands dealing with locals, tried to keep out the visitors by announcing that anyone who took in lodgers would be fined 40 shillings.

Things did not improve and 100 years later, according to old records, the High Street was still attracting rogues and beggars from the Lothians and Lanarkshire like bees to honey. The incomers thought nothing of gatecrashing a local wedding or funeral if it meant free food or drink. An observer at the time commented: "They passed the nights in drinking and other beastlie filthiness".

In 1574 attempts were made once again to confine the traveller - this time at national level. Nobody in Scotland between fourteen and seventy was allowed to beg anywhere except in their own parish. Those who ignored the new law risked being hanged or having their ears nailed to a tree and then cut off. But things never improved - thanks to negligent officers who failed to enforce the law.

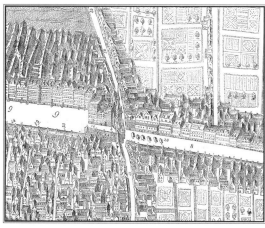

EAST END OF HIGH STREET, NETHERBOW, AND WEST END OF CANONGATE.
(From Gordon of Rothiemay's map.)

The Medicine Murders!

The two worst murderers in the history of Edinburgh found most of their victims in the taverns of the Old Town. They were Burke and Hare, who between Christmas, 1827, and October, 1828, strangled at least sixteen people so that they could sell the bodies to an anatomist for medical research. In the nineteenth century, doctors found it virtually impossible to get specimens, because of the public's attitude to human dissection, and willingly paid out large sums to anyone who could keep them supplied.

Most corpses found their way to the anatomist's table after being taken from the grave by "bodysnatchers" or "The Resurrectionists", as these people were more popularly known. But robbing cemeteries was too much work for Burke and Hare. They found their "specimens" by murdering innocent men and women. The two deliberately chose people who weren't likely to be missed — old tramps, orphans, prostitutes and beggars.

The idea originated from Burke the day his old lodger, a man called Donald, died — still owing a few weeks' back rent. He turned over the lodger's room hoping to find some cash but there was nothing there. Wondering how to cut his losses Burke recalled a recent conversation with

JOHN DOWIE'S TAVERN. *(From the engraving in Hone's "Year Book.")*

some friends about a Dr Knox who was pioneering human dissection at the University. Burke quizzed a few medical students about the doctor — and discovered that Donald's body would be more than appreciated for use in his lectures at the School of Anatomy.

So when night fell Burke put the body in a barrow and wheeled it to Knox's house. He was surprised to find that the famous doctor asked no questions and, happily, made his way home with the proceeds of his evening's work — £7 10 shillings. Burke went to his favourite ale-house and told Hare about his good fortune. Soon they were discussing ways to get more bodies.

One of the first victims was the pretty teenager Mary Patterson. She spent the last night of her life in jail after causing a disturbance while drinking with her friend — 18 year old Janet Brown. On being released in the morning they went to the nearest "spirit shop" for a gill of whisky to refresh themselves. The girls sat beside Burke who was enjoying his regular morning glass of rum and bitter. He soon realised they were easy victims and got them drunk. After an hour Burke suggested they should return to his lodgings for breakfast and the girls readily accepted. But once at the house Janet had a vision of what was about to happen and left. Mary never saw the light of day again. Other victims included a Canongate scavenger, Constantine Burke, and a local idiot, Daft Jamie Wilson.

Many more people were to have a similar fate before the discovery of a woman's body at Knox's house in December, 1828, revealed the practices of these vile men. Soon it was known that at least another fifteen persons had been done to death for dissection, and as the news spread by word of mouth the numbers increased.

The trial of Burke and Hare, two Irishmen who'd worked as labourers on the construction of the Union Canal and toured Scotland selling fish before starting their careers as professional murderers, was fixed for Christmas Eve. Edinburgh was in uproar and thousands of extra newspapers had to be printed to satisfy the hunger for information about the affair.

There were of course heroes - a Mr and Mrs Gray who lodged in one of Burke's rooms. The papers told how the Grays had overheard a conversation between the two murderers concerning plans to dispose of the corpse of a Mrs Docherty, an elderly dear who lived in the room next door. The couple informed the police and next day Knox's house was raided. Mrs Docherty's body was found in a tea chest.

The trial lasted 24 hours. Hare turned King's evidence and later had to flee to Ireland to escape from the furious crowds who wanted to lynch him. Meanwhile, Burke was taken to Calton Jail to await the sentence of the court — execution. Even to the last he was unrepentant. His only complaint as he lay in the cell was that Knox had got off without paying for Mrs

Docherty's body. Needless to say there were few tears shed when an audience of 20,000 watched him being put to death at 8.15am on January 28, 1829. The occasion allowed ordinary folk to show how they felt about the threat posed by ruthless men prepared to cash in on the shortage of specimens — no matter what the price. Hence the reason for such a large turnout.

Indeed the problem of bodysnatching from graves was so bad that iron railings had to be put round graves in many cemeteries and families kept vigils at night in case their loved ones became a target. The outcry was successful because Parliament later passed sweeping new laws which defined clear regulations for dissection. They had the effect of forcing these ghoulish robbers and murderers out of business.

The sensational trial also finished Knox. Although found not guilty of any crime he became a social outcast. Once the most popular and respected lecturer in the anatomy school, he was now snubbed by colleagues and friends. The remainder of his life was spent quietly as a virtual recluse.

OLD HOUSES IN THE WEST PORT, NEAR THE HAUNTS OF BURKE AND HARE, 1869. *(From a drawing by Mrs J. Stewart Smith.)*

Bewitched!

Edinburgh was once a principal centre for 'witchcraft' and old records show that between 1479 and 1722 more than 300 women were burned to death on Castle Hill after being found guilty of "working for the devil". Today a plaque in a wall at the foot of the esplanade, opposite Cannonball House, marks the spot. In the seventeenth and eighteenth centuries the Presbyteries of Scotland, under strong Puritan influence, gave the go-ahead for the burning of hundreds of witches, no matter how flimsy the evidence.

We know today that most of these women had probably never committed a crime in their lives. But it should be remembered that our ancestors were extremely superstitious and truly believed that some seemingly ordinary folk took the form of "old hags" at nightfall, to fly through the air on brooms dispensing evil spells like confetti.

Typical entry in Presbytery records for a witch burning; (1633)

For 10 loads of coal to burn yen *£3 6 8d*
For a tar barrel *14 10d*
For harden to be jumps to them *3 10d*
For making of Ym *8d*

Once a Kirk session and Presbytery were convinced that they had found a witch she was "passed out of ecclesiastical hands to the civil magistrate to be dealt with". Cases were heard in the city by fifteen Lords of Session — but witches were not allowed to give any defence. A minister wrote this description of one such case: "The hag is stripped in court to the waist and if the Devil's marks are seen that is proof that Satan has nipped her person. If she doesn't cry when a needle is inserted into her then that is final proof that she is a witch".

One of the most famous Royal Mile witchcraft stories broke in 1670 but it was centred on a man! He was Major Thomas Weir who for twenty one years had been Captain of the Town Guard. Weir was also a highly respected churchman, because of his ability to quote long Bible passages from memory, and write stirring prayers. Intellectuals and wealthy merchants regarded it a great honour to be invited to the occasional prayer meetings the Captain held at his house in Upper Bow. He was unmarried and lived there with his sister, Grizel.

It was at one such gathering, attended by Sir Andrew Ramsey, the Provost, that Weir paved the way for his death. Members of the audience, prepared for an evening of some good old-time religion, gasped as their host began confessing to every possible kind of crime imaginable — some too horrific for words. Sir Andrew ordered an immediate medical examination,

MAJOR WEIR'S LAND. *(From a measured drawing by T. Hamilton, published in 1830.)*

suspecting that Weir's mind was temporarily unbalanced. But the doctors pronounced him fit in mind and body and more tests, carried out over the following few weeks, produced similar findings. Meanwhile, Weir tossed aside suggestions to withdraw the claims and left the authorities with no alternative but to throw him in the Tolbooth and fix a trial date.

The ordinary folk of Edinburgh were more than ready to believe that the tall, severe-looking head of their Town Guard was guilty. Children were frightened of Weir, who always dressed in black, and it was said that his staff had magic properties which allowed it to move before him completely unaided.

Evidence at the trial was, as usual, more or less meaningless. Weir was con-

THREE CAPTAINS OF THE TOWN GUARD. *(After Kay.)*

victed on: his own ramblings; the
statement of a woman who said that
she had been bewitched by him some
40 years earlier!; a beggar's statement
that Weir rode in a coach down High
Street with the Devil; and a claim by
Grizel that she found "the devil's
mark on his shoulder". So in April,
1670, the unfortunate captain was

THE TOWN GUARD HOUSE.

hanged at the Grassmarket. Most historians feel that Weir probably made the
admissions because of his uncanny ability to foretell events. He could
always predict the results of battles and seemed to feel that this was due to
the fact that some evil spirit "must be in possession of my soul".

Another alleged witch who met her death in the flames at Castle Hill
was also an influential citizen in her time — Dame Euphane MacCalzean,
daughter of a Court of Session judge and owner of a large estate. She was
introduced to the practice by a Catherine Campbell of Canongate.
MacCalzean was found guilty of: (1) Sinking a vessel as it travelled between
Leith and Kinghorn thus causing the deaths of the 60 people aboard; (2)
Along with a group of other witches she had tried to destroy King James
VI's ship as it sailed into North Berwick on the return from Denmark.

THE TOLBOOTH. *(After the painting by A. Nasmyth.)*

But it wasn't just the wealthy who were in on the act. Barbara Napier, a High Street hawker, was burned for casting spells on "gentlewomen". Another hawker, Agnes Fynnie, was put to death in 1643 after being found guilty of depriving twelve people of their speech. In 1661, life got even tougher for the witches of Canongate when the town council gave Baron Bailie William Johnstone sweeping new powers to wipe them out. William unfortunately got rather over-zealous and ended up having half the women thrown on the fire!

Another Canongate incident, some 70 years earlier, resulted in the death of Sir Lewis Bellenden, a Lord of Session. Along with a sorcerer, Richard Graham, he carried out a series of experiments to raise the Devil in his back garden. It supposedly worked — but old Lewis suffered a fatal stroke. The shock was too much for him!

MORAY HOUSE, CANONGATE. *(From a drawing by Shepherd, published in 1829.)*

Miracle vision in the sky

A king's encounter with a killer stag led to the foundation of Holyrood Abbey in the twelfth century.

The story began on the morning of a Holy Rood Day — September 14. David I was staying at Edinburgh Castle and although the day was an important religious festival he ignored pleas from his churchmen to spend the time in prayer and holy worship, preferring instead to go on a hunting trip.

The king loved the thrill of the chase and one of his favourite sporting grounds was Drumsheugh Forest. The thick woodlands were full of deer, foxes and many other members of the animal kingdom.

It was a jolly party the king led out of the castle on that autumn morning so long ago. A chase was soon underway after the footservants had spotted a young deer and forced it to flee.

During the hunt David became separated from his companions. He carried on alone for a while then stopped to have a drink of water from a spring. He was bending down to quench his thirst by the pool's edge when the peace around him was broken by a loud noise from the surrounding

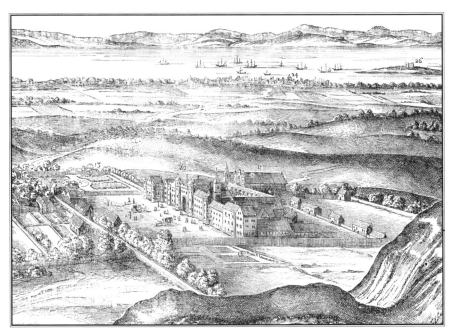

HOLYROOD PALACE AND ABBEY.
(From the rare View, by Hollar, in the British Museum.)

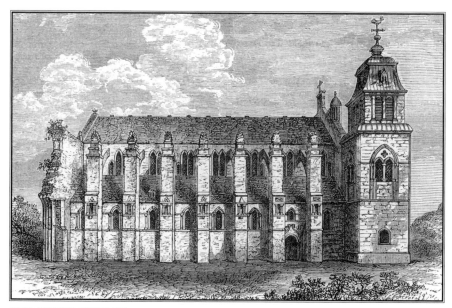

THE ABBEY CHURCH.
(From an engraving in Maitland's "History of Edinburgh".)

bushes.

Then a giant stag appeared before the defenceless king. The beast attacked and its antlers pinned him to the ground. He seemed doomed to die - until a little silver cloud appeared in the sky. As the stag was about to move in for the kill a vision of the cross came from within the cloud. At this the animal reared backwards, turned and fled.

David was naturally in a state of severe shock and it took every ounce of energy he could muster to crawl through the trees in search of his horse. He found it a few minutes later and sounded a call on his horn. This summoned his fellow hunters and when the king told them of his encounter they were dumbfounded.

The king decided to do something as a tribute to God for saving his life. Then later that night St Andrew, Patron Saint of Scotland, appeared at his bedside. David was told to build a church and monastery on the spot where his life had been saved.

The order was of course obeyed and a great clearing was made in the forest. No cost or effort was spared in building an impressive Abbey which was dedicated to the Holy Rood (i.e. cross).

Other buildings were added later and Augustinian monks from St Andrews settled there. The king made sure that they would never want for anything. Gifts of land in various parts of Scotland, together with forestry, fishing and grazing rights in other areas, helped to make Holyrood prosperous. Examples of the perks included: Half of the fishing in Inverleith Harbour; the right to fish for salmon and herring in the Clyde; free grazing for their swine in Stirlingshire Forest and unlimited supplies of timber from the same area free of charge.

They were also allowed to create their own town outside the Abbey walls over which they had complete control.

The monks also operated a sanctuary and Arthur's Seat as well as the Holyrood Park we know today fell within its boundaries. Whilst inside a fellow was safe from his creditors for 24 hours. Apparently at the end of this period the debtor had to apply to the Abbey for permission to leave the park without fear of being hounded further.

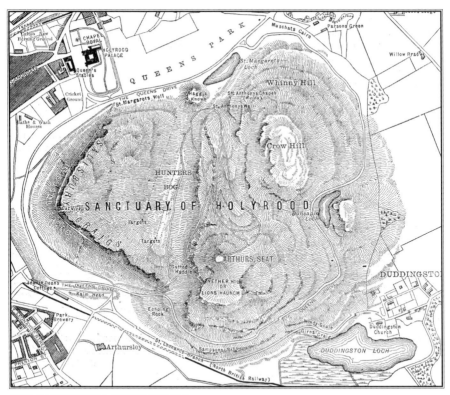

THE SANCTUARY OF HOLYROOD.

Surrender!

In the fifteenth century a rebel Highland chief, under sentence of death after revolting against King James I, decided to give himself up during an important religious service at Holyrood.

Alexander, Lord of the Isles, was wanted for leading an army of 10,000 men on a trail of destruction in which Inverness and much of the surrounding district was destroyed. After defeating his forces in a battle at Lochaber the king announced a reward for information leading to the clansman's arrest.

But Alexander decided to go to the king first. He chose to make his appearance whilst Scotland's leading statesmen and churchmen were attending service to celebrate the festival of St Augustine — patron saint of the Order to which the Abbey belonged.

Members of the congregation gasped in astonishment when the door burst open and a barbaric figure, dressed only in shirt and hose, came thundering in. The stranger, who was soon recognised, made straight for the king, and held out his sword in submission.

James decided to reward this courage by altering the death sentence to a term of imprisonment at Tantallon Castle.

Alexander was later set free and had his castles, lands and honours restored. In fact he became something of a family friend for later the ex-rebel stood sponsor to the king's twin sons who were born at Holyrood and baptised in the Abbey Church.

A Royal bride — aged 12

The first Royal Palace at Holyrood was built for the English bride of King James IV — and she was just 12 years old at the time.

James gave orders that it was to be ready for the arrival of his wife-to-be, Margaret Tudor, who made the seven week journey from London to Edinburgh for the famous marriage of the Thistle and the Rose.

This was perhaps one of the most important events in our nation's history. It was hoped that the union of Scotland's king and the Princess Royal of England would put an end to the national rivalries which had stained the soil of these islands with blood for so long.

As it happened the marriage did not bring peace at the time but it was significant in that the couple were to have a great grandson, James, who inherited the thrones of both countries - an event which was to lead to England and Scotland eventually becoming one nation.

James and Margaret were wed at Holyrood in August, 1503, after she had made the journey from London accompanied by her governess and an escort of Scottish lords. The highest men in the land and their wives, dressed in the richest clothes and jewels, attended the ceremony.

Following the service, which was conducted by the Archbishop of Glasgow and the Archbishop of York, a huge feast was held. For the remainder of the week Edinburgh was in a festive and happy mood. Jousts were held in the Palace grounds for the entertainment of the Royal newly-weds.

Wedding off — so Palace is destroyed

The Monastery, Abbey Church and much of the Palace were destroyed - all because a wedding didn't take place. Henry VIII of England was furious after plans for the betrothal of the infant Princess Mary and Prince Edward fell through.

This happened when the Regent of Scotland changed his policy suddenly after the marriage treaty had been signed and opted to support a French Alliance. The English king hit back with an invasion of Scotland, led by the Earl of Hertford.

The troops came by sea instead of land and when six enemy ships appeared in the Forth the Scots were taken completely by surprise. Edinburgh and the surrounding area were plundered. The Abbey, Holyrood House and the Palace were all burned. This left the monks homeless and they moved away - leaving the Abbey a permanent ruin. Church and Palace were rebuilt.

Four years later, in 1547, the English returned after the Battle of Pinkie to destroy and plunder the church for a second time.

Vicious murder at Palace

A meal in Mary Queen of Scots' supper room at Holyrood Palace on the night of March 9, 1556, ended abruptly with the brutal murder of her personal secretary David Rizzio.

It was a murder which was to shock all Scotland. For this cold blooded killing had been carefully planned by a group of powerful men who regarded Rizzio as a menace in their midst. The murderers included Lord Darnley, Mary's husband; the Earl of Morton, Lord Ruthven and George Douglas.

They decided to act because Rizzio, a court singer who had found favour with Mary, was considered to be too dangerous. He was allowed by Mary to sit in on private consultations which she held with the highest nobles of the land and was a regular guest in her supper room.

One reason for a closeness developing between Rizzio, an Italian described as a 'little mis-shapen, evil-favoured and black featured man' and Mary was the childish antics of Lord Darnley.

Mary and Darnley were married in the Chapel at Holyrood but things soon began to go wrong. He drank too much, had a nasty temper and would be away from the Palace for weeks at a time without letting her know where he was. So it was not surprising that Mary should turn to Rizzio.

When told about their friendship by nobles Darnley became extremely jealous and it didn't take much persuasion to secure his aid in carrying out the murder. On that fateful night the guests at Mary's little supper party included the Duchess of Argyll, the Master of the Household, the Captain of the Guard who was a fellow by the name of Erskine, plus of course Rizzio.

As they ate, drank and laughed sinister things were happening outside. A group of armed men took the Palace keys from the porter as he was locking up for the night. Some of the party were placed as guards at strategic points around the building while the rest went inside by the private door to Lord Darnley's chambers.

By using the connecting stair between these quarters and Mary's rooms they were able to get into the supper chamber unchallenged.

Led by Lord Ruthven the attackers burst into the room. The supper table was knocked over in the confusion. Rizzio grabbed the Queen and begged for mercy. Alas, there was nothing she could do, for George Douglas took the dagger from Darnley's belt and stabbed the terrified Italian. Mary was kept prisoner in the room whilst he was dragged out into the outer hall and callously murdered.

Rizzio's body was stripped of its rich clothing and carried down the

THE QUEEN MARY APARTMENTS, HOLYROOD PALACE.
1. Queen Mary; 2. Supper-room; 3. Bedroom; 4. Private Staircase; 5. Lord Darnley's Room.

THE GALLERY OF THE KINGS, HOLYROOD PALACE, 1880.

stair into the Chapel where he was buried.

While all this was going on Mary was in the room with Darnley who had got half drunk to screw up courage and see through his part in the affair.

It seems that some nobles were keen that Mary should sign a document which would have given this drunken oaf more say in the running of Scotland's affairs. However supporters of the Queen who were in the Palace at the time managed to get out and informed the Lord Provost that Mary was being held prisoner. Immediately the bells of St Giles were sounded, summoning the burghers and craftsmen of Auld Reekie to the Mercat Cross.

The Lord Provost gave them the news and it was immediately agreed to make for Holyrood and demand her freedom. Darnley, as two faced as ever, appeared at a window and assured the crowd that there was nothing wrong. For obvious reasons he wanted to cover-up the exact situation knowing that his own life would be in danger if the truth got out. He managed to persuade Mary to leave Edinburgh with him and at 2am on the 12th they made off for the safety of Dunbar Castle.

The gunpowder plot

Less than a year later Scotland was again rocked by a murder which was a bit too close to Mary for comfort. It happened when a house in which Lord Darnley resided was blown apart in an explosion.

A group of nobles arranged the death and it seems unlikely that Mary didn't know that moves were afoot to end her husband's life. But no-one can say whether or not she took an active part in the scheme.

It had been a difficult year for the Royal marriage. After the death of Rizzio Mary stayed at Stirling then at Edinburgh Castle where her son — later James VI — was born in June. In the autumn she was back at the Palace but Darnley refused to go anywhere with her and announced that he intended going abroad for good. His father, the Earl of Lennox, appealed for a change of heart but he would have been as well talking to a wall.

A meeting of the Privy Council was held and Darnley received a summons to explain his irrational behaviour. Whilst being questioned he suddenly leapt to his feet and declared: "Adieu, you shall not see me for a long space. Adieu, gentlemen". He then walked out of the room. And out of the Palace for the very last time.

But Darnley didn't go abroad. We next hear of him the following January, ill with smallpox and living at his father's home in Glasgow.

Mary visited him and, despite their recent difficulties, the get together went well and they parted on friendly terms. He took up her suggestion to try Edinburgh for a change of air and a special course of baths which were supposed to stop the skin of a smallpox victim being marked by the condition. After a short stay at Craigmillar Castle, which he didn't like, Darnley was taken to Kirk O' Field House. It stood in a garden of its own just outside the city wall and was owned by the Earl of Hamilton.

Mary paid her husband regular visits and he made steady progress. But in the cellars below bags of gunpowder were being smuggled in.

At two o'clock in the morning on Monday, February 10, the peace of the capital and its Royal Palace were shattered by an almighty explosion. The Queen woke up with a start. What on earth could have happened, she wondered. Then the Earls of Bothwell, Argyle, Atholl and Huntly, accompanied by their wives, arrived at her room. It seemed that Kirk O' Field House had been blown apart!

The Earl of Bothwell and a team of Household Guards who were sent to investigate returned to confirm the worst. The house had indeed been destroyed and Darnley's body was found in the garden.

Whatever her previous knowledge of the plot, if any, the tragedy certainly had an effect on the Queen. Suffering from severe mental and physical distress, she was unable to leave her bed for several days.

Darnley's body was embalmed and laid in front of the Holyrood chapel altar. It remained there for five days before being placed in the Royal vault beside the remains of his uncle, James V.

Not surprisingly the good folk of Scotland's capital were asking a lot of awkward questions, with feelings running so high that the funeral had to be kept private to avoid riots breaking out.

Three months later this odd affair took another twist. On her way back from Stirling Mary and her attendants were taken prisoner by the Earl of Bothwell, accompanied by a number of his soldiers.

Six weeks later, on May 15, Mary and Bothwell were married at four o'clock in the morning at the Holyrood Chapel. The kingdom was scandalised. Bothwell had been one of Darnley's murderers. On top of that he'd divorced his beautiful bride of only 15 months — Lady Jean Gordon — in order to be free to marry the Queen.

After three weeks at Holyrood the pair were forced to flee to the security of Borthwick Castle after a number of nobles decided to declare war on the Queen and march on Edinburgh. Later, to avoid unnecessary bloodshed, Mary gave herself up, but Bothwell ran.

And so the young Queen, who in August, 1561, had arrived from France amidst great excitement was now taken to begin her imprisonment at Lochleven Castle and never again did she enjoy the court life and luxuries of Holyrood.

A trickster exposed!

Just a month after David Rizzio's assassination at Holyrood his brother Joseph arrived in Edinburgh — and brought shame to the Italian family's name by being exposed as the key figure in a web of fraud and robbery.

It is understood that Queen Mary sent for him to fill the office which had been held by David. He was installed at the Palace as her private secretary and given all the perks and status of a senior member of the Royal Household.

Sadly, however, Joseph chose not to be loyal to the Queen who had placed so much trust and faith in him. He used the power and influence of his position to try and get rich. A fellow Italian, Joseph Lutini, who held a junior servant's post on Mary's staff, was ensnared into the schemes.

Lutini stood as guarantor when Rizzio borrowed 100 crowns from a city moneylender. This cash was to be used to finance robberies. As security Lutini offered his own personal credit and stable of valuable horses. The moneylender became suspicious and on making a quick check discovered that the servant didn't own a single nag and was completely broke. He was furious at this deception and reported the whole matter to the Queen.

Mary wasted no time in asking Rizzio for a full explanation. The other servant at this time was in Berwick en route for a period of convalescence in Italy which the Queen had arranged to help him get over a recent illness. Our cunning plotter seized the opportunity to blame the fraudulent scheme on Lutini, whom he also accused of stealing a large sum of money.

Mary wasn't taken in. For a while she had had a suspicion about the disappearance of a pair of her valuable bracelets. She now openly accused Rizzio of theft. He broke down, but again put the blame on his associate.

The Queen wrote to Sir William Drury, Marshall of Berwick, and asked for her servant to be detained and returned to Edinburgh with an escort. Under cross examination by the law chief Lutini protested his innocence. A subsequent search of his possessions revealed an astonishing letter written to him by Rizzio. In it the rogue admitted double-crossing him in front of the Queen and suggested that he should stick to the story that had been put to her for the sake of the country's honour!

Just as justice was about to catch up with Rizzio a tragedy occurred which allowed him to leave these shores a free man. For while Lutini and an escort were travelling up from Berwick with the vital evidence Darnley was assassinated, throwing Edinburgh and the Royal Court into a state of confusion and controversy.

Rizzio quietly faded from the scene and made his getaway to Italy — probably with the Queen's bracelets in his possession.

She bathed in wine!

While at the Palace Mary had a somewhat bizarre habit. She bathed in red wine!

Perhaps this was an extension of Cleopatra's liking for a scrub in asses' milk. At least if Mary accidentally swallowed some of the tub's contents the experience wouldn't have been unpleasant.

Mary also enjoyed dressing up as a man and wandering the streets of Edinburgh to get first hand experience of the lifestyles and talking points amongst ordinary mortals.

Her interests included billiards, golf and dice.

THE HOLYROOD DAIRY. *(From a Calotype by Dr. Thomas Keith.)*

Campaign of terror

A campaign of terror forced King James VI to quit Holyrood in December, 1596, and move the entire Court to Linlithgow. This proved a real blow to Edinburgh and its future prosperity was seriously threatened.

Trouble started after the Earl of Bothwell, nephew of Mary's husband, was imprisoned for his part in an alleged witchcraft plot to end the king's life. Later the earl, who seems to have been as mad as James was superstitious, escaped and devoted all his energies to organising murder schemes. It would seem that after each attempt the Head of State was prepared to forgive him.

However the strain of all this, coupled with pressure from the extreme Protestant party about his religious beliefs, drove James to leave town.

The folk of Edinburgh were in a panic about their future as trade was bound to slump without the presence of Royalty and the wheels of Government. The Reforming Party realised that they should make their apologies and James was given a firm promise that they would be better behaved in future.

So, thus, were differences mended and the Royal Court returned to Edinburgh on New Year's Day. Seven years later the Palace was again the scene of drama. On March 26, 1603, a horseman arrived with news that the king's cousin — Queen Elizabeth of England - - was dead.

The rider, Sir Robert Carey, had a ring from Lady Scrape, a member of the London Royal household. James had given her the ring on a previous occasion with the instruction that it was to be sent to Edinburgh when Elizabeth passed away.

Ten days later James set off to claim the English throne and promised to return to Scotland every three years. As things turned out fourteen years had elapsed before he came back.

This wasn't the only promise which he didn't keep. Sir Robert Carey was assured a handsome reward for being first with the news of Elizabeth but in the excitement of taking over the English throne James forgot all about him.

Mob stole dead royals

Bones of the dead were stolen from their coffins and scattered on the ground by an angry Edinburgh mob. They were on the warpath over a decision by King James VII to turn the abbey church at Holyrood into a place of Catholic worship.

James, a devout Roman Catholic, made his declaration after coming to the throne in 1685, but things were to change when he was later forced to give up the crown and go abroad after the thrones of England and Scotland were offered to William and Mary of Orange.

INTERIOR OF THE CHAPEL ROYAL OF HOLYROOD HOUSE, 1687.
(After Wyck and P. Mazell.)

The Duke of Gordon continued to hold the Palace for James and ignored a command from the Privy Council to get out. Eventually the City Guard managed to gain access through the back and forced him to surrender.

The mob moved in. In the king's private chapel books, ornaments and vestments were destroyed. The Chapel Royal, their next target, was left a complete ruin. Then the Royal Vault was broken into. Lids were ripped off coffins and bones were scattered all over the place.

An inspection of the bodies in the coffins had been made a few years before this dreadful raid so it was possible to know whose bones were disturbed.

A report of the inspection mentions: "King James ye fyft of Scotland", Queen Mary's father, whose body was measured as being well over seven feet. Other coffins contained the remains of Magdalene of France, Prince Arthur, third son of James IV, Arthur, Duke of Albany, second son of James VI, Lord Darnley and a Countess of Argyle.

In 1898 Queen Victoria had as many of these remains as possible collected and placed in one large coffin in the Chapel Royal with an inscription giving the names of those who had been removed.

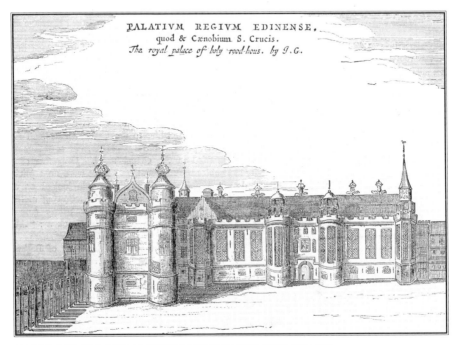

HOLYROOD PALACE AS IT WAS BEFORE THE FIRE OF 1650.

Retreat!

On September 15, 1745, the good folk of Edinburgh were at Sunday morning service singing the praises of the Lord and listening to words of wisdom from the Good Book when their worship was suddenly interrupted by startling news. Bonnie Prince Charlie and his rebels were marching on the capital!

Worshippers who had heard the alarm bells found two companies of dragoons, the city guard and a detachment of volunteers being assembled to face the Highlanders who were reported to be within sight of the town boundary at Duddingston.

The dragoons went into action but after an initial brush with Charlie's men retreated in terror. The next move was to lock all the town gates.

The Prince, however, rode in via Holyrood Park wearing a short tartan coat, scarlet breeches, military boots and a flat green velvet bonnet with a white cockade. At the Palace he was met by crashing debris from a tower which had just been hit by a cannonball. No one was injured and, quite unconcerned, young Stewart strode into the Palace to cheers from his supporters.

That night a grand ball was held. No doubt all the beautiful young ladies were keeping their fingers crossed that Charlie would ask them to dance.

PRINCE CHARLIE'S HOUSE, DUDDINGSTON. *(From an engraving in the Roxburgh Edition of "Waverley," published by Messrs. A. & C. Black.)*

Two days later Charlie's men marched to Prestonpans where they defeated the troops of Sir John Cope. Then he returned to Holyrood and remained there until the end of the next month. A Council of War was held at 10am each day, and the Prince visited his troops at their Duddingston camp each afternoon.

Later however came the fatal decision to invade England and finally the tragedy of Culloden. This battle ended the Second Jacobite Rebellion and young Stewart's hopes of becoming king.

So in little more than six months after Charlie's entry into Edinburgh we find the Duke of Cumberland residing at Holyrood on his way south after triumphing at Culloden. He even slept in the very bed which the Young Pretender used. Things had turned full circle.

A ROYAL EDINBURGH VOLUNTEER.

THE GUARD HOUSE AND BLACK TURNPIKE.

Mysteries of Arthur's Seat

Arthur's Seat, situated in Holyrood Park, is at 822 feet the highest of the seven hills on which Edinburgh is built. It is said to be named after King Arthur who reigned over Strathclyde from 508 to 542. Another theory is that the name is a corruption of the Gaelic, *Ard-na-Said* or Height of Arrows. There could be something in this if one considers the suitability of the area for archery.

Hundreds of years ago much of the park was thick woodland which provided robbers with excellent hideouts. A hiker accidentally stumbled on one such place while out for a ramble in 1728. Access from a shallow pit led to a completely fitted out room inside Salisbury Crags. The walls were lined with skins.

The park has three different names and this often leads to confusion on the part of visitors. Besides Holyrood it is known as Queen's Park or King's Park. The latter comes from James V who first enclosed it *circa* 1540.

This area has been below the sea several times. The rocks, once thousands of feet high, were crunched by great glaciers which left the marks we see today.

On a lighter note it is interesting to recall that Arthur's Seat was a favourite spot for our troubled Royal ancestor, Mary Queen of Scots. In 1564 she held an open-air banquet to celebrate the forthcoming marriage of John, Lord Fleming, to Elizabeth, heiress of Robert of Ross.

In these modern times May Day is observed with a sunrise service at the top of the hill. It's thought that the custom had its origin in a pre-Christian ceremony of sun worship. Today's lassies hope to improve their beauty by washing their faces in the morning dew.

Arthur's Seat was often used as an important signal base. A beacon on the summit was the quickest way of sending a message to Fife that the "auld enemy" from across the Border was approaching.

At Hunter's Bog, under the shadow of the hill, Bonnie Prince Charlie encamped his men in 1745 before riding over the crest of the hill to take up residence at the Palace.

A bizarre discovery was made on Arthur's Seat in 1836. On the north-eastern slopes seventeen small coffins, each containing a neatly carved "corpse" dressed in correctly fitting clothes, were uncovered.

Their origins and meanings are a mystery to this day. They could be the relics of ritual burials for persons lost at sea, or perhaps some kind of witchcraft symbols.

Victims of the plague

Holyrood Park became a mass grave four centuries ago — after many of Edinburgh's citizens died from a highly infectious disease.
The capital was thrown into a panic in April, 1645, when cases of the plague were confirmed. In an effort to check the outbreak the town council erected huts in the park for the reception and shelter of victims. Dr Joannes Paulitius, who was paid £80 Scots a month, worked night and day attending to her patients but it was inevitable that lives would be lost.

All the victims were laid to rest in the surrounding ground.

In the eighteenth century townsfolk dug up the body of a murderer which had been buried in the park and tossed it about like a football. The 'game' ended with the corpse being thrown over Salisbury Crags.

The body was that of poacher Murdo Campbell who killed the Earl of Eglinton on the seashore at Ardrossan on October 24, 1769. Campbell, who oddly enough was an excise officer by profession, flew into a rage on being caught red-handed and when the Earl asked him to hand over the gun he shot him.

The murderer was brought to Edinburgh for trial and sentenced to death. But before the hangman could get a rope around his neck Campbell committed suicide in the Tolbooth Prison.

This was regarded as an act of cowardice by the local population who no doubt also felt a bit cheated at missing the spectacle of an execution. So when the body was buried the following day at the foot of Salisbury Crags they formed a mob and went to dig it up.

Campbell's remains were later recovered by some friends who disposed of them in the Firth of Forth.

In the days of yesteryear boarders at Heriot's Hospital had an interesting custom when they were marched through the park en route to bathing at Portobello. A stone was always laid on Muschat's Cairn - and thus yet another murder story was kept alive.

For it was at the spot where surgeon Nicol Muschat murdered his wife. This happened towards the end of 1720 and followed earlier attempts to get rid of her by divorce and poisoning.

Mrs Muschat had been delighted when he invited her to go for an evening stroll but joy turned to terror when the surgeon threw her to the ground and slit her throat open.

His sole motive was that he had become tired of the woman. His punishment was death by hanging.

Many a duel of honour was fought in the park despite laws which strictly banned such confrontations. An old diary records that "on March 11,

1579, William Gluffer and James Hepburne slew one another at the singell-combat, on the hill callit Saint Leonardis Craigis. The said twa ver buriet on the morne thairefter".

On Sunday April 20, 1600, a duel had been arranged between Robert Auchmuty, a surgeon-barber and burgess of Edinburgh, and James Wauchope, whose father was a merchant burgess. This followed an argument which had taken place on the previous day.

But the confrontation was anything but fair. For Auchmuty had the support of friends who attacked James, "and crewallie, with swords, straik him in the face and vpoune the held, and gaif him foure bludy woundis thairon; and thairbye maist barborouslie, crewallie and tyrannouslie slew the said vmqle James Vauchope, vpoune set purpois, provisioune and foirthocht fellonye in his contemptioune etc".

Auchmuty was subsequently tried and sentenced to death. An attempt to escape from his cell in the Tolbooth by using an acid to eat through the bars was foiled.

On Saturday May 27, 1615, a student by the name of John Brand stabbed a William King to death and in punishment for this had his head chopped off at the Mercat Cross.

More than half a century later, on June 17, 1669, William Mackay, a tailor, and a soldier friend were having a drink at Edinburgh Castle. But the alcohol had the effect of turning the good natured natter into an argument.

Things got so out of hand that the two decided to fight a duel in the park and on the way there borrowed a couple of swords. In what proved to be a fair fight the soldier was slain.

Later Mr Mackay found himself under arrest and subsequently at the wrong end of the hangman's rope.

Humble beginnings

Worshippers who attend service at St Giles include Her Majesty the Queen, leading statesmen, visitors from far off lands and citizens from all walks of life who have their homes in Scotland's capital. The place breathes history, little wonder when you consider there has been a church on this site for over 1,000 years.

Chronicles tell us that "Edwinsburch" had its own parish church as early as 854. The congregation would have consisted of a few folk who lived in thatched huts situated around the simple wooden building. The church belonged to the Monastery of Lindisfarne which in its turn had been founded by the monks of Iona.

For a century or two a stone built church stood on the site and this was later replaced by a massive Norman edifice which was erected by Alexander I in 1120.

Here, in 1384, a secret meeting was held of the knights and barons of Scotland to plan an attack on England. It was agreed that French mercenaries should be used in the fight. The meeting was held amidst maximum security conditions because the King, Robert II, wanted peace and would have firmly opposed the plan.

SEAL OF ST. GILES. *(After Henry Laing.)*

The nobles went ahead and systematically burned and looted towns and villages in the north of England. But in the following year Richard II took his revenge by leading a strong army into Scotland. Dryburgh and Melrose Abbeys were destroyed. Edinburgh was attacked. The town and St Giles were burned. Only the Abbey and Monastery of Holyrood escaped.

Of the church all that remained standing were a few pillars. A few years later rebuilding work began and the costs had to be met through sacrifices on the part of many ordinary folk. The king gave the building fund

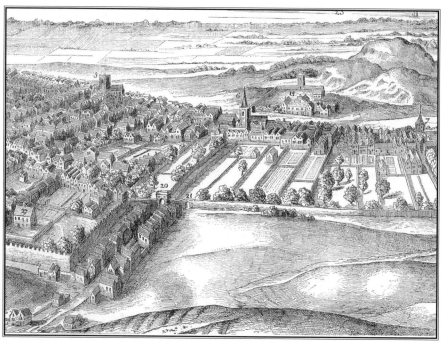

EDINBURGH, FROM ST. GILES'S CHURCH TO THE CANONGATE.
(From the rare engraving by Hollar, in the British Museum.)

all the proceeds from fines levied for certain offences. These included tradesmen who had been found guilty of using light or faulty measures and apprentice boys who were found playing cards in working hours.

The building and extensions to the church took place over 150 years. In the fifteenth century St Giles was made a collegiate church, thereby raising it to the status of a cathedral.

Starved to death

A man who cruelly starved his nephew to death in the dungeon of a castle had a troubled conscience for the rest of his life. Each new morning brought a reminder to Robert, Duke of Albany, of the terrible deed for which he had been responsible.

So after the destruction of the Cathedral in the attack by Richard II he decided to make a practical demonstration of remorse by donating a side aisle to the new building. Archibald, Earl of Douglas, one of his close associates, helped with the costs. Both men had been responsible for starving David Duke of Rothesay, at Falkland in 1402 after he had been put into their care. They had been fortunate indeed to escape serious punishment for this cruel deed.

It was common practice in those days for wealthy men to seek forgiveness in the eyes of God for serious crimes by making gifts such as this.

EDINBURGH, FROM THE KING'S BASTION, 1825.

Miracles of St Giles

St Giles Cathedral takes its name from a renowned medieval saint who performed many miracles. He is understood to have been born at Athens in 640 and to have died sometime between 720 and 725, on the first Sunday in September. For centuries this date was regarded as one of the most important on Edinburgh's calendar and an annual procession was held through the streets in his honour.

Egidius, to give St Giles his Latin name, is thought to have performed his first miracle by placing his coat over a sick man he met on the way to church. This had the effect of producing an immediate and total recovery.

Later a special prayer saved the life of a fellow who had been subjected to a deadly serpent bite. On another occasion a service was interrupted by the screams of a man whose body had been possessed by an evil spirit. Egidius drove it out by using his extraordinary gifts.

All this brought fame but he preferred anonymity and was constantly on the move around Europe in search of peace. A cave in the Gothic forest near Nimes provided the perfect sanctuary. Here he lived on roots, herbs and the milk of a hind.

One day the hind was chased by hounds belonging to the King of France and driven into the cave. There Giles was discovered. Later, when he told his story, the king decided to erect a monastery nearby and gave him the title of abbot. He held the title until his death.

One of the most interesting works to be compiled on the cathedral and the saint's life was written by William Chambers in 1879.

Mr Chambers says: "Numerous churches and other ecclesiastical establishments, also hospitals, were founded in his honour. In England alone there were 146 churches dedicated to St Giles.

"His fame having reached Edinburgh, he was adopted as the patron saint of the church".

During the reign of James II an arm bone, said to be that of St Giles, was brought to Scotland and gifted to the church. This was enshrined in silver and kept among the treasures of the church until the Reformation.

In July, 1557, it disappeared during the night and according to John Knox was 'drowned in the Nor' Loch and afterwards burnt'.

Despite the loss it was decided to hold the annual St Giles parade as usual in 1558. A substitute relic was borrowed from the Grey Friars but in the course of the day a riot broke out and it was vandalised by a mob.

Times of trouble

In 1559, during the Reformation controversy when attempts were being made to smash the ways of the Roman Catholic Church, a message was sent to councillors. It came from the Queen Regent, Mary of Lorraine, in the summer of that year and it asked them to do all in their power to guard religious places against attacks from mobs.

As a result of this 60 soldiers were stationed outside the church. Crosses, altar furnishings, candlesticks, vessels for Holy Communion, alms-dishes, etc. were taken from the various chapels and hidden in private houses for safe-keeping until the danger was over.

Protestant nobles pulled down some of the altars at St Giles and Mass was scrapped. A few months later French soldiers, sent by the Guises, arrived at Leith and their presence swung the balance of power in favour of Catholics. However the status quo was restored when English troops came to the assistance of the Protestant nobles and forced the French to return home.

This time St Giles was completely stripped. Sailors' ladders and ropes were used for the operation. The beautiful carvings were smashed to pieces with hammers and ripped out. Gold and silver ornaments, jewellery, priceless church plate, and valuable brasses and hangings were confiscated. All they left behind were bare walls and the roof support pillars. The entire interior was whitewashed.

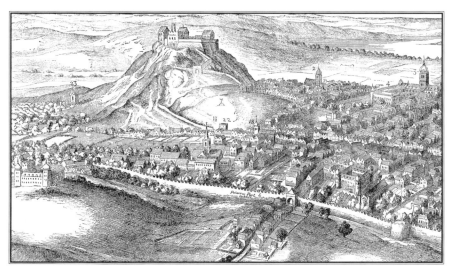

EDINBURGH, FROM ST. CUTHBERT'S TO ST. GILES.
(From the very rare view by Hollar, 1670.)

John Knox

John Knox is the most famous of all the St Giles preachers. He played a key role in the theological storm which went on until the Reformation of the Scottish church in 1560. Following that Knox was made pastor of this famous Royal Mile religious institution.

William Chambers' history of St Giles says: "In starting afresh after the recent clearing out the church must have presented an empty desolate appearance.

"At that period there were no fixed pews. The seats were chairs or wooden stools, provided chiefly by worshippers for their own accommodation. The bulk of the people stood, and they would gladly stand for hours listening to their favourite preacher. Knox often preached, it is said, to three thousand persons.

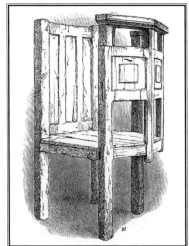

JOHN KNOX'S PULPIT, ST. GILES.

"The work he went through was immense. He preached twice on Sunday, and three times every other day of the week, besides attending to other clerical duties".

Knox was born at the East Lothian village of Gifford in 1505 and after being educated at Glasgow University he became a priest around the year 1530. Some 15 years after that he switched to the Protestant faith and in 1547 was re-ordained as a minister of the Reformed Church.

But later Knox was taken prisoner by the French, the emissaries of the Guises, and condemned to a living hell on the gal-

JOHN KNOX'S HOUSE. *(From a drawing by T. Allom.)*

leys for two years. This was followed by a 19-month spell in jail at Rouen.

The Reformer was a minister in Geneva before returning to Scotland to take up the St Giles post. He hated the Catholic church and used every ounce of his energy to attack it — and its prominent members — whenever the opportunity arose. Queen Mary was one of his principal targets and she had to suffer many insults from his abrasive tongue. Whilst Knox thundered from the pulpit she had the rites of her own church performed in the private chapel of Holyrood.

Knox was paid more than Court of Session judges — £44 English money a year - and had a fully furnished manse further down the High Street which is still there to this day and open to visitors.

His church was the scene of excitement when a struggle broke out for the post of Regent of Scotland after the assassination at Linlithgow of James Stewart, Earl of of Murray - 'The Good Regent'. The Earl of Lennox, paternal grandfather of the young king, James VI, was the chosen favourite much to the annoyance of Sir William Kircaldy of Grange, the Governor of Edinburgh Castle.

He had until then been loyal to the king's party but after that switched to the party of the exiled Mary and started a civil war. Sir William fortified Edinburgh and on March 28, 1571, placed a military force on the roof and steeple of St Giles as a show of strength to citizens.

Local craftsmen replied to this move by breaking into the church and threatening to pull down the roof support pillars. Kircaldy's men attempted to counter this by making holes in the vaulted ceiling and opening fire on the attackers.

Calderwood, the church historian, says they 'made the vaute like a riddle to shoot through'.

In between these two events Knox had died. He preached his last sermon on November 9, 1572, and passed away a fortnight later. Knox lies buried somewhere in Parliament Square.

KNOX'S BEDROOM.   KNOX'S STUDY.

Market Place

The area around St Giles was, for a long time, the centre of Edinburgh's shopping market. Traders arrived at first light and stayed until darkness fell. Housewives of all classes pushed and jostled amongst the stalls for their purchases of bread, meat, milk, vegetables and so on.

Surrounding inns advertised eel pies and fresh trout from the Nor' Loch (now Princes Street Gardens) and the Newhaven and Musselburgh fishwives came here to sell their oysters, mussels and fish. Lady Nairne fashioned their sellers' call into a song that is still popular to this day:

Wha'll buy my caller herrin'?
They're bonnie fish an' halesome farin',
Wha'll buy my caller herrin'
New drawn frae the Forth?

Wha'll buy my caller herrin'?
O ye may ca' them vulgar farin'
Wives an' mithers, maist despairin'
Ca' them lives o' men.

THE HEART OF MIDLOTHIAN.
(After the print published in 1852 by Messrs. W. & A.K. Johnston.)

Eventually there were so many traders crowding around St Giles that the magistrates took action by fixing certain places where each trade could do business. Thus we had the likes of Candlemakers' Row, Shoemakers' Land, Bakehouse Close, Grassmarket and Lawnmarket.

ST GILES'S CHURCH IN 1878.

Buried under the floor

In the late sixteenth and early seventeenth centuries there was a dramatic rise in Edinburgh's population. Because of this St Giles was portioned off and became a grammar school, courts of justice, a police office, town clerk's office, weaver's workshop and even a prison. The apparatus for public executions was kept in one corner.

Later, as the need for churches increased, St Giles was divided into four separate kirks, each with its own congregation. At the middle of the eighteenth century the list of churches were: The Choir or High Church in the east; The Tolbooth Church in the south - west; and the Old Church in the middle and part of the southside. Another portion was still used as a police station until well into the nineteenth century.

INTERIOR OF THE HIGH CHURCH, ST. GILES.
(From a nineteenth century engraving.)

James Graham, Marquis of Montrose, found his way to his final resting place under somewhat peculiar circumstances. Says Chambers: "He distinguished himself as a military commander in cause of royalty during the civil war. Montrose's history is well known. Captured and brought into Edinbugh, he was condemned and executed on May 21, 1650.

"His body was dismembered. His limbs were sent to different parts of Scotland, while his head was stuck on a spike on the Tolbooth.

"After the Restoration, the scattered remains were collected with tokens of respect, and deposited in the Abbey of Holyrood. Thence they were brought by a solemn funeral procession, at which the magistrates of Edinburgh assisted, and entombed in St Giles on May 14, 1661".

While Lord Provost of Edinburgh between 1865-1869 Chambers often attended public worship at St Giles with the other Magistrates and members of the Town Council.

Recalling such occasions as the visit of George IV to Edinburgh in 1822 and the General Assemblies of the nineteenth century, Chambers says: "There was a distressing mustiness in the atmosphere, which ventilation failed to remedy, for the ground was saturated with human remains, which ought long since to have been removed as dangerous to the health of the congregation".

It was while attending service at St Giles that William Chambers, a brilliant and wealthy publisher, hit on the idea of launching an effort to restore the building to the beauty and dignity which it had enjoyed in a bygone age. He later gave a large sum of money to a restoration fund and asked others to subscribe.

During twelve years of hard work the dividing walls were removed, pillars were dug out of the plaster which encased them, broken or chipped stones were

THE NORMAN DOORWAY, ST. GILES, WHICH WAS DESTROYED TOWARDS THE END OF THE EIGHTEENTH CENTURY.
(From a drawing by Armour, c1799.)

repaired and the covering of plaster which obscured the roof was removed. The floor was dug through to a depth of several feet. An immense quantity of human remains were removed in hearses for burial in a churchyard.

On May 23, 1883, a large congregation gathered for the opening service. Sadly William Chambers was not there. He had died two days earlier.

THE LAWNMARKET, FROM ST. GILES, 1825.

THE CITY CROSS IN THE NINETEENTH CENTURY.

MEETING OF THE GENERAL ASSEMBLY OF THE CHURCH OF SCOTLAND IN
THE OLD KIRK, ST. GILES CATHEDRAL, 1787. *(After a drawing by David Allan.)*

Library pioneer

Allan Ramsay caused a rumpus in 1725 by opening a lending library in the neighbourhood of the Luckenbooths at St Giles. Wodrow, the Calvinist, complained about the "villainous, profane and obscene books" but the library survived and flourished.

Sir Walter Scott took great delight in poring over the library's 30,000 volumes. London booksellers, worried by its popularity, tried to get the library closed down but after a series of costly legal actions they had to admit defeat.

Two owners spanned the period between the departure of Ramsay and the arrival of William Creech who from there published the books of most leading writers of his day including Burns and Adam Smith. Two literary journals, *The Mirror* and *The Lounger*, were issued from here and enjoyed a keen following. Important matters of the age were discussed in the coffee room which made up part of the premises.

ALLAN RAMSAY'S SHOP, HIGH STREET.

Jenny Geddes riot

An old Edinburgh market woman by the name of Jenny Geddes threw a stool at the Dean of St Giles during morning service — and sparked off a storm which rocked the entire country. As a result of the incident churches were closed, all preaching in Edinburgh was suspended for several weeks and the smouldering flames of religious revolt soon erupted in a blaze.

The cause of all this trouble was Charles I, a staunch Episcopalian, who came to Edinburgh for his Scottish crown in 1633. He was determined to force the English style of church government on the Scots and also make them use the prayer book which was a feature of services south of the Border. His first step was to constitute Edinburgh a Bishopric. St Giles became a cathedral church and Bishop Forbes was the first bishop followed later by Bishop Lindsay.

Auld Reekie's folk were not amused. They felt that all this smacked of Popery. Feelings were running very high indeed when on July 23, 1637, the first new style service was held.

Three years after creating the cathedral Charles sent orders that the Book of Common Order, introduced by John Knox and greatly loved by the people, was to be replaced by the English liturgy.

The usual prayers were read out at the start by Mr Henderson, a faithful servant of the congregation for some years. He ended his part of the proceedings with tears in his eyes and declared emotionally: "Adieu, good people, for I think this is the last time I shall read prayers in this place".

Now it was time for Bishop Lindsay to occupy the pulpit and Mr Hanna, the Dean, seated himself at the reader's desk just below. The new prayer book was opened and Hanna began reading from it. There was much muttering and moaning from the congregation. The Dean couldn't help but overhear some of the remarks which were being directed at him, "craftie-fox", "Ill-hanged thief" and "Judas" amongst them.

But it was Jenny Geddes who took the lead in doing something positive. In those days it was common for folk to take their own stools to church. Jenny, red with anger, picked up her stool and threw it at the Dean declaring: "Traitor! dost thou say Mass at my lug?"

Hanna managed to duck in time, then the service had to be abandoned completely after other stools came hurtling through the air. Outside Bishop Lindsay was dragged from his carriage as he tried to leave. He could have ended up dead but for the presence of some friends who succeeded in getting him away.

Following this riot there was a demand for the withdrawal of the offending liturgy. Charles I refused to budge so the following February the National Covenant was signed in the Old Greyfriars Churchyard. And thus began the long and bitter struggle between the Covenanters and forces of the Crown.

Doubt has been placed on the authenticity of Jenny Geddes. One historian says she was in fact Barbara Hamilton, wife of a local merchant. It's also pointed out that 30 years passed before the stool incident first appeared in print and only then in the form of a somewhat sarcastic English poem.

Another argument is that there was a Jenny Geddes who sold vegetables by the Tron Kirk some 23 years later in 1660. This was the year of Charles II's Restoration. Jenny was one of the most active people involved in the celebrations and won the title "Princess of the Tron Adventures". Non-believers ask how she could have taken part in a riot which opposed the king of the day in 1637. This is a fair point, although one should remember that a lot of time had passed. Also such was the closeness of living in the Edinburgh of those days that it would have been difficult for most people not to have been involved in the great enthusiasm and excitement which the Restoration produced.

THE OLD TRON CHURCH. *(From an engraving in Arnot's "History of Edinburgh.")*

Witches and old villages

The **800** acre site on which the New Town is built has an exciting and stirring past. Witches were once tried in what is now Princes Street Gardens and burned to death on ground we know today as Picardy Place.

Only a few centuries ago the thoroughfares which house the shopping and business centres of our modern capital were lonely country lanes which residents of the Old Town wouldn't dream of using after dark.

Highway robbery and murder were not uncommon. But justice was swift. For example one man had his hands cut off on being arrested for killing two children, then 24 hours later was hanged before a large crowd.

Scattered over the area were farms, hamlets and several large villages. All the evidence suggests that folk have lived on this land since ancient times.

In the summer of 1822 workmen digging the foundations of a house on the west side of Royal Circus discovered a Pictish grave. It was surrounded by flat stones and the form of a skeleton was still visible when it was opened. But the remains crumbled to dust when touched. A year later several rough stone coffins were found during a similar work in Saxe-Coburg Place.

Construction of the New Town meant that the independent communities outside the old walled city, which had survived countless raids and loootings during time of war, were swept away.

Moutrie's Hill, occupying land now graced by Register House and St James' Centre, was a typical victim of progress. The families who lived in its trim little cottages had a commanding view over unspoiled country to the Forth and Fife.

Several theories have been put forward to suggest the origin of the name Moutrie. One expert thought that the derivation was from Moutries "which is supposed to be the corruption of two Gaelic words signifying the covert or receptable of the wild boar".

However it is generally put down to the fact that a wealthy fellow called Moutray had a mansion there. His family were leading lights during the reign of James V.

Nearby, at the former General Post Office, was Dingwall Castle, a square keep with towers at right angles. The builder was John Dingwall, one of the original judges of the Court of Session.

Next door stood a leper hospital where hundreds must have met a painful death. An entry in records dated September 30, 1584, states that Michael Chisholm and others were commissioned to inquire into "the estait

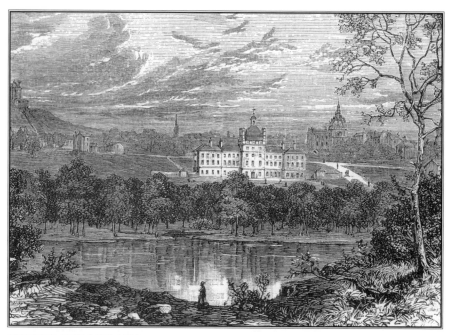

THE BURGH LOCH, 1880.

and ordour of the awld fundatioun of th Lipperhous besyde Dyngwall".

From Moutrie to the middle of George Street there used to be a lovers' lane called Gabriel's Road which was a favourite spot for walking long before any plans were made for an enlarged Edinburgh. The name survived well into the nineteenth century even though most of it had vanished with the building of new houses.

In that fascinating book *Memorials of Edinburgh* we read: "This was a country road along which citizens wended their way between green hedges which skirted the pleasant meadows and corn-fields of Wood's farm, and which was in days of yore a favourite trysting place for lovers, where they breathed out their tender tale of passion beneath the fragrant hawthorn".

Romantic words, but this same thoroughfare also witnessed violence for it was the scene of that bloody murder which we briefly referred to earlier.

The facts were simple. Teacher Robert Irvine was employed by a wealthy couple to educate their two young sons. But he got involved with the family maid and lessons were neglected while the couple took every chance they could to be together. When the brothers uncovered his secret they threatened to inform their parents.

Robert knew that he and the girl would be instantly dismissed and

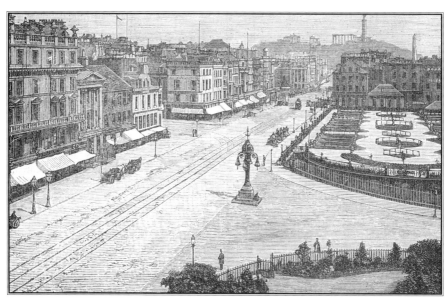

PRINCES STREET, LOOKING EAST FROM THE SCOTT MONUMENT, 1880.

NELSON'S MONUMENT, CALTON HILL, FROM PRINCES STREET.
(From a drawing by A. Nasmyth, published in 1806).

thrown out into the beggar-infested streets with only the clothes they stood up in. So he asked the boys to accompany him on a walk along Gabriel's Road to talk things over, and once out of sight of Moutrie's Hill he stabbed them both.

However, Irvine did not realise that a party of ramblers, who'd stopped nearby for a picnic, had seen everything. The amorous master was arrested and his hands cut off with the knife he'd used to murder his pupils.

On hearing the facts the Baron of Broughton, who owned the land and power over life and death on it, gave orders that Irvine was to be executed. In those days the word of the baron was final.

While the decision was perhaps justified in this case the system led to many unfair practices.

Our forefathers were extremely superstitious and would brand women they didn't like as witches on the flimsiest of evidence.

These unfortunate creatures appeared before the baron in his tolbooth (on the ground now occupied by the east end of Barony Street) and could find themselves under sentence of death for having a wart on their hand or a hooked nose.

A Scottish Privy Council minute of December 1, 1608, reveals that the Earl of Mar expressed concern over the way supposed witches were

THE OLD CHURCH OF ST. CUTHBERT'S, AND THE NOR LOCH, 1880.

being treated at Broughton.

It goes on to mention one specific incident which shocked Mar: "Convicted, they were burned quick, after such a cruel manner, that some of them died in despair renouncing and blaspheming God; and others, half burned, broke out of the fire and were quick cast in again, till they were burned to death".

An Act of Parliament in 1746 ended the dictatorial powers of the baron and paved the way for our modern democratic system of justice.

It is interesting to note that the burgh of Broughton is mentioned in the foundation charter for Holyrood Abbey granted in 1128 by David I. In later centuries its rows of thatched houses with roughly built forestairs and tiny windows contrasted strangely with the fine buildings of the advancing New Town.

Meanwhile witchcraft was also linked with the Nor Loch, later drained so that Princes Street Gardens could be laid. During the reign of James VI suspected witches were put through the ordeal of "trial by water". If they drowned then obviously the devil was NOT in possession of their soul but if the women floated to the surface then they were considered evil and burned at the stake on Castlehill!

A typical case was that of poor Elsie Peat, a perfectly honest and law abiding citizen. She was kept afloat by her clothes which acted as a buoy. Anyone watching must have known that she was saved by the simple laws of gravity. Nevertheless Elsie was still thrown on the fire.

The murky dark waters were the scene of many suicides. According to records 150 people took their lives here. Several references exist to the story about a shoemaker who waded out into the loch watched by a large crowd. They urged him not to be so foolish but their shouts annoyed a wealthy gent whose home stood nearby. He opened his window and yelled: "What's all the noise about? Canna ye e'en let the honest man gang tae the dei'l his ain gait?"

The Nor Loch had other uses too. Citizens caught eels and water rats as well as dumping their rubbish in it. In a way it's remarkable that this spot should now be such a scene of beauty — in the shape of Princes Street Gardens.

A long road ran by the Nor Loch from Moutrie to the village of Silvermills — this busy thoroughfare was bordered by two stone walls and known as the "Lang Dyke" or "Lang Gate". Roughly speaking it followed the route of our modern Princes Street.

Silvermills flourished through James IV's hobby of hunting for pre-cious metals believed to be present in great abundance in the Scottish soil. What's left of this once-bustling community is now buried beneath St Stephen's Church and the surrounding streets.

One reference to the village written by an Edinburgh man many generations ago states: "We can remember many a Saturday ramble through green fields which ended at this rural hamlet".

On the site of Picardy Place until the late eighteenth century stood the village of Picardy. This was occupied by weavers who were apparently brought over from the French province of that name by the British Linen Company. Another story suggests they were a group of refugees who found their way to Scotland and settled on what was then common ground.

Charlotte Square was occupied by the mansion and grounds of a George Lockhart whose daughter was said to be possessed by an evil spirit.

Records state: "A person alive in 1824 said that, when a child, he saw her climb up to the top of an old fashioned four poster bed. In her fits it was impossible to control her".

On the other side of the New Town, not far from Saint Andrew Square, was Greenside. Land here was gifted to the capital by the king for use as a tournaments stadium.

Had history developed slightly differently this name might still be in common use today. For when the Union Canal was first projected engineers planned to run it through the valley of the Nor Loch and over to Greenside, where another man-made waterway would be opened to link up with the Forth by Leith. A giant harbour was to be built near the Calton Hill so that ships could come right into the heart of the New Town.

Perhaps it's fortunate that this scheme never got off the ground.

ST. ANDREW'S SQUARE, 1880.

Battles of Princes Street

After the second unsuccessful Jacobite Rebellion of 1745, which had attempted to smash the union of the Scottish and English Parliaments, a new era of peace and prosperity spread over Britain.

Towns no longer needed gates and walls to keep out enemies. Overcrowded Edinburgh was able to breathe a sigh of relief. The population of 25,000 in 1700 had doubled by the middle of the century and there was no way to grow within the traditional boundaries.

So in 1766 Parliament gave the go-ahead for an extension of the limits. Council chiefs organised a competition on how a new town should be built and it was won by architect James Craig.

He produced a gridiron plan which started and finished with enclosed squares. This was the first piece of deliberate town planning in the country and even names were specially chosen. George Street was named after the king; Queen Street in honour of his consort; and Princes Street after the Prince of Wales. The narrower streets between — Thistle Street and Rose Street — recognised the emblems of Scotland and England. Patron saints were remembered in St Andrew's Square and St George's Square (now Charlotte Square).

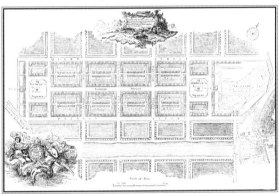

CRAIG'S PLAN OF THE NEW STREETS AND SQUARES INTENDED FOR THE CITY OF EDINBURGH.

Not all these names were contained in Craig's original plan. Princes Street was first proposed as South Street, then St Giles Street. On hearing the latter suggestion George III remarked that it would "sound ill in English ears". This was because the St Giles district of London was a badly rundown slum area at the time.

According to another account the king was heard to say: "What? What? St Giles Street? Never do! Never do!" Diplomatically, Prince's Street was suggested and in later years the apostrophe vanished to give the spelling we know today.

The plan also had George Street as the main thoroughfare with Princes Street, lined by a long row of plain houses, as a side street.

THE NORTH BRIDGE AND THE BANK OF SCOTLAND.
(From a drawing by Sir John Carr, published in 1809.)

An important step towards the drawings on paper becoming reality was taken in October, 1763 when the foundation stone of the first North Bridge was laid so that citizens could gain easy access to the green fields that are now the city centre.

Four years later advertisements invited plans "by which buildings might be erected in the most regular handsome, and commodious manner".

But folk were not keen to reply. A new development on such a scale was an uncharted sea and builders and tradesmen were reluctant to move. The civic fathers introduced an incentive by offering a £20 prize to the first man who built a house in the New Town. It was won by Mr John Young, who made his home at Thistle Court, off Saint Andrew Square.

Silk mercer John Neale put up the first house in Princes Street in 1769 - and was relieved of paying city rates. Some sources say this was another carrot offered by councillors while one states that he lived rates free in return for giving up land that was vital to the success of the development.

Despite the attempts to end this practice the waiver continued until modern times when Edinburgh Corporation bought the property from the old London and North Eastern Railway Company. They paid £110,000 and re-sold at a public auction a short time later making £11,000 profit.

Neale wasn't the only early proprietor who didn't miss a trick. According to one popular story an eminent eighteenth century lawyer who lived in Saint Andrew Square built a house at 40 Princes Street so that his view of the clockface on St Giles wouldn't be blocked. Apparently he liked to be punctual about his duties at Parliament House. In 1937 representatives of this gent's succesors made an unsuccessful attempt in court to halt plans for a bigger building planned on the site by new owners.

Building of Princes Street was completed in 1805 and rubbish gathered during excavation work in this and other streets was dumped in the Nor Loch, which eventually vanished. The pile of muck also helped create another access to the houses via the Mound.

The Gardens which were laid on the reclaimed land are now open to everyone but at first were jealously guarded by the old proprietors as a private retreat. Perhaps this is understandable as families had spent thousands of pounds from their own pockets on planting them.

And we've a lot to thank these folk for. In 1771 they took out a 99-year lease on the site after magistrates discussed a scheme to build houses down both sides of Princes Street. Lord Cockburn described this as an "absolutely insane project" and won support from a group of advocates who succeeded in getting a statute which prohibited the closing up of the street.

"Those who remember the battle have scarcely drawn their breath freely since", wrote Cockburn later.

Owner occupiers had a key which cost £1 to get into their beloved gardens but an unscrupulous Rose Street locksmith upset the apple cart by producing replicas. And the builder of houses in Castle Terrace provided his buyers with keys which just happened to fit the gates as well!

It was strictly forbidden to lend keys and gifts were only made on the rarest of occasions. Sir Walter Scott, who did get one legitimately, remarked: "A great treat as I am too tender hoofed for the stones". (A reference to old cobbled streets).

But the shortage of a key didn't put some folk off. One old book tells us that ladies out for their afternoon stroll had to "dart for cover from those dreadful creatures of the New Club who smoked cigars".

Boys who played cricket and stole strawberries didn't help while the gardener caused offence by keeping pigs. Officers from the castle exercised their dogs and servants armed with baskets of clothes were continually coming and going from the bleaching green.

The original aim of the gardens — "where genteel folk might walk at all times with freedom and without risk of meeting improper persons" — began finally to crumble in 1851 when the Scottish Association for Suppressing Drunkenness called for public access on Christmas and New Year's Day "to keep people from the dram shops".

Then the castle band began playing at twice weekly sessions and as soon as this attraction caught on they threatened to stop unless everyone was allowed in. Eventually the proprietors reluctantly agreed but notices went up warning "the lower orders" to "know your place and keep out".

THE SCOTT MONUMENT, PRINCES STREET.

Ghosts, worthies and scandal

An amazing woman who scandalised Rose Street and had to be thrown out of town by order of court, the boys who made a strange pact with their blood, the saga of the performing ghosts and the cash disaster that nearly ruined Sir Walter Scott are just some of the stories we feature in this chapter, which looks at the many characters who've lived in the New Town over the past two centuries.

Obviously interesting people are as important to a town's development as buildings and this former asset has never been in short supply in the modern capital.

Sir Walter Scott, who did a great deal through his romantic novels and poems to improve the standing of Scotland in international eyes, was brought up at 75 George Street where his mother died.

She was described by a contemporary as "a woman possessed of superior natural talents with good taste for music, poetry, and a great conversationalist".

At 25 George Street young Scott received his first education in a somewhat rowdy school. He wrote in later years: "Our next door neighbour,

GEORGE STREET IN THE 1880s.

Lady Gumming, sent a note to beg that the boys might not all be flogged at the same hour, as though she had no doubt that the punishment was deserved, yet the noise was dreadful".

He finished his scholastic career at the Royal High School and on marrying went to live with his new wife at 108 George Street.

The landlady was shocked by the writer's habit of using the best rooms, normally reserved for Sunday, on ordinary working days. In those times the street consisted largely of three storey houses which were favoured by folk who wanted something quiet away from the bustle of Princes Street.

Under council rules buildings weren't to be more than 48 feet above ground level and failure to comply meant a £30 fine and immediate removal.

While George Street brought immense happiness to Sir Walter 10 Princes Street was an address that didn't. For in January, 1826, it was disclosed that publisher Archibald Constable, with whom he had close business links, was in debt to the tune of £250,000.

After hearing the news Sir Walter wrote: "Naked we entered the world and naked we leave it, blessed be the name of the Lord!

"Things are so much worse with Constable than apprehended that I shall never save Abbotsford (his huge home in the Borders) or anything else.

"I feel neither dishonoured nor broken down by the bad — now really very bad — news I have received".

Constable, who surprised Edinburgh by paying up to £3,000 a time for a single poem, had risen from being a lad in a city bookstore to head of the local publishing and book sales trade in a very short period of time.

After the crash Sir Walter embarked on a massive writing programme through the Waverley novels and managed to clear off his debts. The fact that he had written them was one of the literary world's best kept secrets.

One woman guessed the identity of the anonymous novelist before Scott told all at a gathering in the Assembly Rooms on February 23, 1827. Her name was Catherine Sinclair.

An author, she was a member of the famed Abbotsford circle and today a small monument can be seen at North Charlotte Street which was put up in her honour.

A few weeks before the announcement Catherine handed Scott a covered painting draped in cloth with a label reading "The Great Unknown" attached. Sir Walter removed the cover and saw himself, but only smiled.

Catherine was a good hearted lady who did a lot of work for charity. She introduced workers' canteens to Edinburgh where meals were served costing the equivalent of one and a half new pence and paid for the first street water fountain so that thirsty drivers and their horses could get a drink.

George Street has many other links with Scotland's literary past.

The publisher of the Edinburgh edition of Robert Burns' poems lived at number 5, while another close friend of the Bard, James Ferrier, principal clerk of session, had a house near St Andrews Church.

The poet Percy Shelley and his 16-year-old sweetheart, Harriet Westbrook, got lodgings here after they ran away from their homes in England to wed. Both were under age, according to English law, but found a preacher willing to marry them in the shape of the Rev Joseph Robertson of Leith Wynd Chapel. This was in 1813 and the couple spent a five week honeymoon in Edinburgh.

A few years later, when deep in debt, Shelley again brought his wife to the capital so that they could escape from creditors. This time their base was at 36 Frederick Street.

· Sir Henry Raeburn, a poor boy from Stockbridge who became a famous portrait painter, set up his first studio at 18 George Street in 1787. He stayed there for over 10 years before moving to York Place.

Sir John Sinclair, who compiled the first Statistical Account of Scotland which paved the way for our modern census, has connections with the thoroughfare. He was married with fifteen children who were all over six feet tall and lived there for many years. The section of pavement outside his front door was nicknamed "Giants' Causeway".

Running parallel with George Street is Queen Street — Sir James Y. Simpson lived at number 52. As professor of midwifery at the University and the man who developed the use of anaesthetics his home was a meeting place for men of letters and science from all over the world.

Simpson came from a humble family in Bathgate but he never sought to kick over the traces of his upbringing and once established was a generous man who gave willingly to the poor.

By experimenting on himself and two friends he finally became satisfied on November 28, 1847, that

SIR JAMES YOUNG SIMPSON.

QUEEN STREET, 1880.

chloroform was safe to use in operations.

This fine citizen died from heart trouble on May 6, 1870, and a crowd of over 1,700 people from all parts of Britain assembled at Queen Street for the funeral.

Unfortunately the departure of another local worthy — under quite different circumstances — wasn't mourned by such a big audience.

We refer to a lady known simply as Miss Burns, the daughter of a wealthy businessman from County Durham who lost all after getting divorced and making a disastrous second marriage.

Penniless, his daughters were left to make their own way in the world and the youngest arrived in Edinburgh about 1789 — then a beautiful girl of some 20 summers. Her looks and "the length to which she carried the extravagant mode of her dress" (quote from a journal of the day) assured Miss Burns a lot of attention from young men during her evening promenades along Princes Street.

But goings-on at her home in Rose Street brought a storm of complaints from a group of neighbours — led by a certain Lord Swinton, whose back windows looked onto hers.

These culminated in a court case heard by Bailie — later Lord Provost — Creech whose dislike of Miss Burns was well known. He ordered her to get out of Edinburgh immediately. Should she dare return the penalty would be six months in the House of Correction, a 'drumming' through the streets, then expulsion again.

She appealed to the Court of Session, and, after one refusal, eventually won her case to stay in the capital.

The affair led to a lot of satirical comments being made in newspapers against the character of the bailie. One London journal went so far as to suggest that he was about to lead Miss Burns to the altar — a report which didn't go down too well with Creech. He wrote to the editor demanding an apology — which was duly published.

"In a former number we noticed the intended marriage between Bailie Creech of Edinburgh and the beautiful Miss Burns of the same place.

"We have now the authority of that gentleman to say that the proposed marriage is not to take place, matters having been otherwise arranged, to the mutual satisfaction of both parties and their respective friends".

That she was a famous lady is in no doubt — even Burns put pen to paper and wrote:

"Cease, ye prudes, your envious railing:
Lovely Burns has charms — confess:
True it is she had one failing:
Had a woman ever less!"

While on the subject of naughtiness let us tell you a tale which led to the birth of Jenners, the great Princes Street store. One April afternoon in 1838 two young drapery assistants, Charles Kennington and Charles Jenner, asked their boss for the following day off so they could attend the races at Musselburgh. He refused. They went and got fired.

But a few weeks later they took space in a local newspaper to announce: "Kennington and Jenner will open their new establishment at 47 Princes Street on Tuesday, May 1".

It soon built up a roaring trade. Kennington died in 1863 but his partner continued to build the business and eighteen years later retired as owner of Scotland's biggest retail shop.

However all has not been plain sailing in the history of this Edinburgh institution. Disaster struck on the night of November 26, 1892, when a fire destroyed the premises and £250,000 worth of stock. Some 120 employees who lived there escaped with only the clothes they wore but they were put up at a top hotel and paid full wages plus compensation for lost belongings.

Soon afterwards the job of rebuilding began and on May 6 1895, the new Jenners store opened for business.

Another famous Edinburgh name is the Royal High School which used to be situated in Regent Road, by the east end of Princes Street.

A former pupil, celebrated historian and statesman Lord Brougham, tells of a weird pact he made with a fellow student in an autobiography published in 1862.

"Frequently we discussed many grave subjects including the immortality of the soul and a future state", he wrote.

"The question and the possibility of the dead appearing to the living were the subjects of much speculation and we actually committed the folly of drawing up an agreement written with our blood, to the effect that whichever of us died first should appear to the other and thus solve any doubts we had entertained of life after death".

Brougham goes on to say that after leaving university they lost touch. His friend took up a Civil Service post in India: as time passed memory of the pact faded from his mind.

Then one day, while on a tour of Sweden, the noble lord got the shock of his life.

His friend suddenly appeared before him, stayed for a few seconds, then vanished.

"This vision produced such a shock that I had no inclination to talk about it but the impression made upon me was too vivid to be easily forgotten" said Brougham who recorded the date of the eerie incident as December 19, 1799.

When he returned to Scotland a letter was waiting which contained news that his pal had died - on December 19.

Tales are also centred on the old Theatre Royal, situated on the site of the former GPO building, and a flat in Rothesay Place.

Ghosts used to re-enact plays on stage after the manager and his family had retired to their beds in the flat above. The story of these phantom performers is mentioned in a pamphlet published in May, 1859, to mark the theatre's closure.

At Rothesay Place strange disturbances were reported when the owner took delivery of a piece of wood gifted from a friend's cottage in the north of Scotland. Ornaments flew and fell on the table, drawers opened and closed without anyone touching them, the air in rooms suddenly became heavy with the odour of a strange tobacco.

All these occurrences are linked with a sailor called Merry Jack Tar who haunted the house for years.

Murder most foul!

An evil schoolmaster who had a smart house in George Street caused a sensation in Edinburgh when he was found guilty of murdering his wife.
The case, heard at the High Court in 1878, revealed a remarkable relationship between Eugene Chantrelle, a good looking cultured Frenchman, and his pretty wife, Elizabeth Dyer, daughter of a commercial traveller.

They first met at Newington Academy where he was a teacher and she was one of the pupils. Love blossomed but the couple had to marry in 1868 after Elizabeth, then 16, found that she was pregnant.

They had four sons and their ten years of married life were spent in George Street, first at number 95 and then at 81, scene of the tragedy.

From the outset Eugene, a brilliant academic and author of several text books, treated his wife with contempt. He used to beat her frequently and locked her out of the house at nights.

Desperate, she made many pleas to her parents for help but these fell on deaf ears. Because of the social attitudes of the age they couldn't face the thought of divorce.

Things were so bad that one day Elizabeth wrote to her mother while on holiday at Portobello.

"Well mama if you do not want me to be murdered outright you must see that all I can do is leave him at once. I am sorry to trouble you but if he murders me you might be sorry not to have heard from me".

Mum thought — wrongly — that her daughter was overstating the case, and not long afterwards the killing was carried out in a most cold blooded way.

Chantrelle, a native of Nantes and son of a shipowner, was found guilty of poisoning her by giving opium planted in an orange "and perhaps otherwise".

He said she'd been poisoned by gas which had escaped from a leaking pipe but this was later proved to be untrue by a thorough examination of the body.

A short time before executing his plans the schoolmaster had taken out a £1,000 insurance policy on Elizabeth's life.

When the verdict was announced Edinburgh was full of excitement. Oddly enough many thought that he should be allowed to go free and meetings were held to protest against the sentence - death by the rope. But justice stood firm and Chantrelle was hanged at the Calton Jail on May 31, 1878.

Another interesting murder story is linked with the New Town street of Buckingham Terrace. A gifted student who'd been taking money from his mother's bank account appeared in court in 1926 charged with murdering her and uttering forged cheques. The first charge was found not proven but the second one stood. He maintained that she'd killed herself. The nineteen year old was sentenced to only 12 months in jail.

However, over the next 27 years the son was in and out of prison on a variety of offences including smuggling. He committed bigamy twice and robbed the second victim of her life savings.

Then he met and married a woman who ran an old folks' home with her mother at Ealing, London. He hit on the idea of getting a big insurance pay-out by drowning his latest wife in the bath. But the old lady caught him virtually red handed coming out of the toilet, so he murdered her as well.

At his wits' end the mixed-up soul fled to Germany and later was found in a wood at Cologne. He was returned to London for trial where a coroner's jury, after a retirement of 37 minutes, unanimously found him guilty of both murders.

CHARLOTTE SQUARE, SHOWING ST. GEORGE'S CHURCH, 1880.

A tour of the Royal Mile

EDINBURGH CASTLE

Our tour of the Royal Mile begins at the Castle — there has been a place of defence on this site for 1,400 years.

The castle rock is formed by the core of an extinct volcano. St Margaret's Chapel, in memory of Queen Margaret who died at the castle in 1093, is the oldest surviving building. It is thought to have been built after 1124 when her youngest son David became king. The castle we see today dates from the reigns of James IV and his successors.

In the early 1500s a Great Hall was built out on a massive sub-structure along the south side of the Castle. Then in 1544 an artillery bastion was constructed in front of the cross-wall to increase defences after an English attack. Twenty nine years later the walls were blown apart when Kirkcaldy of Grange attempted to hold it for Queen Mary. New defences included an artillery platform — the Half Moon Battery — and a greatly strengthened

THE ROYAL LODGING OR PALACE, FROM THE GRAND PARADE,1885.

cross-wall. A new gatehouse — known today as the Portcullis Gate — was built.

In later periods came the New Barracks (1796) which accommodated soldiers fighting against France, and important restoration of the Great Hall and Portcullis Gate (1880s). The last major building work was in the 1920s, when the Scottish National War Memorial was constructed.

Some details now about specific parts of the Castle as the visitor comes to them.

ESPLANADE:
Parade ground formed here in the mid-eighteenth century. The land was levelled with waste materials used in the construction of Royal Exchange (now City Chambers). The ornamental walls which run along each side were built in 1816 and 1820.

GATEHOUSE:
Built 1887. Design was cosmetic rather than practical as defence was no longer a prime consideration. In 1929 statues of Robert the Bruce and William Wallace were added on either side of the entrance.

PORTCULLIS GATE:
Situated at head of the approach road. This was the main gateway of the Castle as reconstructed in the 1570s. The upper stages of the gate date from 1886 and replace a simple eighteenth century roof.

ARGYLE BATTERY:
To the right of Portcullis Gate. Also known as the six gun battery, this was built in the 1730s for General Wade, best known as a designer of roads and military bridges.

MILL'S MOUNT BATTERY:
One o'clock gun is fired from here daily. When built the New Town, which they face on now, was open fields.

THE LOW DEFENCE:
May date from the 1540s although in their present form they are seventeenth/eighteenth century.

GOVERNOR'S HOUSE:
1742. Now mainly used as the Officers' Mess of the Castle garrison. Governor's official residence now occupies the right wing only.

THE HOSPITAL:
Remodelled from earlier buildings in the 1890s for medical use.

WESTERN DEFENCES:
Built at two different levels from at least the seventeenth century onwards.

BUTTS BATTERY:
The bow butts, where archers practiced firing at their targets, was in this area, hence the name. These south side defences date from 1708 and 1713 in their present form.

OLD BACK PARADE:
Now overshadowed by the barracks built in the 1790s.

DURY'S BATTERY:
Named after Theodore Dury who rebuilt the Castle's southern walls in the early eighteenth century.

MILITARY PRISON:
1842. Offenders from all Scottish garrisons were kept in solitary confinement here. It was last used in 1923.

THE FRENCH PRISONS:
Where captured French soldiers from the wars of the eighteenth and nineteenth centuries were kept. Some of the graffiti scrawled by prisoners can still be seen. The famous cannon Mons Meg, made in the 1440s, is now kept here as protection against the weather. After a long service of use it burst when firing a salute in 1681, and was then abandoned.

HAWK HILL:
This area is the second highest point of the Castle. Features include the Governor's House and new Barracks.

CROWN SQUARE:
At the heart of the late mediaeval Castle although of the four buildings which now define the Square only two have recognisably mediaeval work in them.

SCOTTISH NATIONAL WAR MEMORIAL:
An eighteenth century building which was transformed in 1927 as a tribute to Scots who fell in the First World War. Stained glass in the windows and a casket containing the names of the dead are prominent interior features.

SCOTTISH UNITED SERVICES MUSEUM:
Erected soon after 1708, this building was originally designed as accommodation for officers.

GREAT HALL:
Since ancient times the main communal living area of the castle was here. Present hall dates from the reign of King James IV and was designed more as a grand place for Royal occasions. The Hall was lit by windows on the south side. The King and members of his Court took their places at the East End. Over the centuries it was subdivided as floors and walls were inserted to provide barracks. Between 1887 and 1891 the Hall was restored to its original splendour complete with elaborate open-timber roof.

THE PALACE:
In a small ground-floor chamber here Mary Queen of Scots gave birth to the future James VI. In a second room the Scottish Regalia of Crown, Sword and Sceptre were stored and walled-up after the Union with England in 1707. In 1818 the vault was re-opened and the Regalia placed on display.

ROOM IN EDINBURGH CASTLE IN WHICH JAMES VI WAS BORN.

ST MARGARET'S CHAPEL:

As already stated this is the oldest surviving structure to be seen in the Castle. At the west end, through the arch, is a semicircular vaulted apse to contain the altar, whilst the main body of the chapel is the rectangular nave, for the congregation.

Leaving the Castle we come to:

CANNONBALL HOUSE:

Edinburgh's first piped water supply was introduced here in 1681 with Comiston Springs supplying the Castlehill Reservoir. A ball in the wall of this house (Castle Wynd North steps, right) marks the gravitation height of the supply. According to a traditional story the ball was fired from a cannon at the Castle towards Holyroodhouse, occupied at the time by Bonnie Prince Charlie.

WITCHES FOUNTAIN:

Opposite side of Esplanade. Marks the spot where 'witches' were once burned at the stake - by and large ordinary women who were innocent victims of crude superstition.

OUTLOOK TOWER:

Lower part of the building was the seventeenth century home of the Laird of Cockpen. Today it is an excellent book and craft centre. Sir Patrick Geddes, the celebrated town planner, was another ex-resident and an exhibition of his work is on display. A Camera Obscura is housed at the top of the building. It was installed in the 1850s for an experiment in optics and updated with a new lens and mirror system in 1945. A novel feature for visitors is provided by the camera operator who can be seen to put his hand over the moving street and lift off cars and people he doesn't like!

MYLNE'S COURT:

One of the first open squares in the Old Town (1690) it was reconstructed by the University in the late 1960s to provide student accommodation. This work won a Saltire Society Award. The Court derives its name from Robert Mylne, the Master Mason to Charles II who built an extension to Holyrood and repaired the Castle in 1689.

JAMES COURT:

Home to philosopher David Hume before he moved to the New Town. Dr Johnson and Adam Smith were entertained here by James Boswell during the grand tour of 1773. James Brownhill, a wright, built the courtyard around 1725, hence the name.

GLADSTONE'S LAND, 1880.

GLADSTONE'S LAND:

Superb example of seventeenth century town house now in the ownership of the National Trust for Scotland and open for all to see. Thomas Gledstanes, merchant and distant ancestor of the Victorian Premier William Gladstone, bought the property on December 20, 1617. The Gledstanes are thought to have occupied the third floor for one of the features of the ceiling is a painted hawk — in Scots, a gled — from which the surname is derived. In 1980 Gladstone's Land was arranged as a seventeenth century merchant's house, the ground floor being set up as a cloth merchant's booth of the period and the first floor as it might have been when occupied in the latter part of that era. There are excellent examples of contemporary paintings and period furniture including a fine oak four-post bed.

LADY STAIR'S HOUSE (1622) AND CLOSE:

Lady Stair was widow of John Dalrymple who played prominent parts in the Treaty of Union and the Massacre of Glencoe. Now a museum for the relics of Robert Burns, Sir Walter Scott and Robert Louis Stevenson.

RIDDLE'S COURT:

Across the way. Name derived from builder George Riddell, a burgess of the city, who was shot dead in 1595 when Royal High School pupils rioted. His house in the courtyard has a turret staircase outside and the inside features lovely sixteenth and seventeenth century painted beams and finely moulded ceilings. A lavish banquet was held here in 1598 for James VI and his Queen, Anne of Denmark.

BRODIE'S CLOSE:

A little further down on the same side. Once the house of the infamous Deacon William Brodie whose lifestyle inspired Stevenson's *Dr Jekyll and Mr Hyde*. By day Brodie was a respected town councillor who championed all that was decent and fair and just; come nightfall however, and he changed into a callous burglar who thought nothing of robbing even the poor and infirm. He was caught red handed breaking into the Excise Office but managed to escape to Holland. Swift recapture followed and he was hanged, ironically, on gallows which he had invented!

DEACON BRODIE. *(After Kay.)*

High Street begins close to the junction with the Mound and George IV Bridge. To the left of these crossroads is the City Chambers; to the right Parliament House, St Giles Cathedral and the Heart of Midlothian, the Mercat Cross and the Tron Kirk.

ST GILES CATHEDRAL:
The origins of this High Kirk of Scotland and many stories connected with it have been told elsewhere in this book. Strictly speaking it has not been a Cathedral since 1688 when the title of Bishop was abolished. The impressive Gothic interior houses many historical monuments and memorials including the Chapel of the Most Ancient and Most Noble Order of the Thistle, the tombs of Argyll and Montrose, and a memorial to Robert Louis Stevenson. The Thistle Chapel, with its superbly carved interior, is described as the most ornate building of its kind built in Scotland since the Middle Ages.

HEART OF MIDLOTHIAN:
This sett of cobblestones near the Cathedral's West Door, in the design of a heart, mark what was the entrance to the Old Tolbooth (City Prison). Scott's novel of the same name made the spot famous. The prison was demolished in 1817 but the heavy wooden door can still be seen at his mansion, Abbotsford. The Tolbooth was originally a place for collecting tolls and in its time served as a meeting place of the Scots Parliament, as Town Hall, Chambers for the Privy Council, and a College of Justice.

MERCAT CROSS:
On the east side of St Giles. Once a site for executions. Nowadays the Lord Lyon King of Arms reads royal proclamations from here.

PARLIAMENT HOUSE:
The Scottish Parliament met here from 1639 until the Union with England in 1707. (Sittings prior to 1639 were in the Great Hall of the Castle). It is now home to the country's supreme Civil and Criminal Courts and the Advocates' Library. Each weekday the magnificent hammer-beam roofed Parliament Hall is filled with the buzz of advocates, solicitors and clients conducting business. An equestrian portrait of Charles II in lead, situated outside in Parliament Square, is Edinburgh's oldest statue.

CITY CHAMBERS:
Designed by John Adam. Built 1753. Described as 'the genesis of classical Edinburgh... the design nucleus from which the New Town was born'. The building, planned as the Royal Exchange, was largely spurned by the merchants who preferred conducting their business in the more convivial surroundings of the taverns. It became the City Chambers in 1811.

ANCHOR CLOSE:
Next to the City Chambers. William Smellie published the *Encyclopaedia Britannica* here in 1768 and the first Edinburgh edition of Burns' poems in 1787. The Bard's favourite hostelry, Dawney Douglas's Anchor Tavern, was nearby.

TRON KIRK:
The name is derived from a weighing beam which stood on the site to check merchants' goods. Today short measures can result in action being taken by the Trading Standards Department and, in due course, a court appearance. In times past justice was more swift - offenders had their ears nailed to the beam! The Tron was originally used by a St Giles congregation displaced in 1633 when that church was made into a Cathedral by royal charter. The building is no longer used for worship.

OLD ST PAUL'S CHURCH:
Episcopalians worshipped in a wool store which stood on the site following their expulsion from St Giles in 1689. The church we see today is a nineteenth century building with a highly dramatic interior. Allan Ramsay opened Edinburgh's first regular theatre in the close (1736) but it was not granted a licence and had to shut soon after. John Spottiswoode, the Archbishop of St Andrews who crowned King Charles I at Holyrood in 1633 and became Lord Chancellor of Scotland two years later, had a house here.

JOHN KNOX'S HOUSE:
Circa 1490. The great Reformer Knox is said to have lived here between 1561-72 although there are those who will debate otherwise. A museum featuring items associated with him is open to the public. Overhanging wooden upper floors and the crow-stepped gable end which faces the street are eye catching features. An outside stair was added in the sixteenth century when the house was sub-divided. Incredibly, town planning authorities tried to have it demolished in 1849 to widen the High Street!

THE NETHERBOW PORT, FROM THE HIGH STREET.

NETHERBOW:
Edinburgh ended here in the days when Canongate was a separate burgh and a gateway marked the boundary. The Church of Scotland Arts Centre, which occupies the site, was opened in 1972 and is designed in the style of an Old Edinburgh town house. Features include a small theatre, the Scottish Storytelling Centre and exhibition space. It is now linked directly to John Knox's House. High Street ends at the crossroad below the Centre where brass plates inset in the roadway mark the outline of the last Netherbow Port, one of the city's six gates. Criminals' heads were exhibited on spikes above the gate - a far cry from today's 'Welcome to the Festival City' signs!

MORAY HOUSE:
Signatories to the Treaty of Union were forced to flee from a summerhouse in the garden and take shelter in Union Cellar, High Street, after being besieged by an angry mob in 1707. In the previous century Cromwell had stayed here on two occasions. From the balcony of the house the Marquess of Argyll, on the day of his son's wedding, looked down on Montrose as he was wheeled to his execution. Now part of the College of Education which takes its name, Moray House was built by the Dowager Countess of Home in 1625. Charles I was a frequent visitor.

HUNTLY HOUSE:
This restored town dwelling of 1517 is now the city's principal museum of local history and illustrates Edinburgh's life down the ages. Items on display include a copy of the National Covenant signed at Greyfriars Churchyard in 1638. The name seems to derive from the fact that the Duchess of Gordon, a member of the Huntly family, had a flat here in the eighteenth century. It is sometimes known as the Speaking House because of four sixteenth century plaques displayed on the front of the building. These are said to answer any criticisms which may be levelled at the building's splendour and, translated, read:

1. Today for me, tomorrow for thee, why therefore carest thou?
2. As thou art master of thy tongue, so also am I master of my ears.
3. The affair of mortals to a steadfast mind is as a shadow.
4. There is hope of another life.

On restoration of the building in 1932 a plaque was added with the inscription: I am old but renew my youth.

ACHESON HOUSE:
Next door to Huntly House, it dates from the early seventeenth century when it was built as a town house for Sir Archibald Acheson, Secretary of State. Robert Hurd, a noted Edinburgh architect, restored the building in 1937.

CANONGATE TOLBOOTH (1591):

The civic centre of Canongate when it was a separate burgh. A hall on the first floor served as both council chamber and court house. Cells for offenders were below. It is now The People's Story Museum, telling of the health, welfare, work and leisure of citizens.

CANONGATE KIRK (1688):

Originally built for King James II to serve the congregation from the church of Holyroodhouse which the King wished to turn into a Chapel Royal. Famous people buried in the churchyard include economist Adam Smith; Edinburgh poet Robert Fergusson and Robert Burns' 'Clarinda', Mrs Agnes McLehose. Thirteen years after Fergusson's death in 1774 Burns provided funds to have a headstone erected at the grave. On the front of the stone is inscribed the Bard's own verse:

> *No sculptured Marble here nor pompous lay*
> *No storied Urn nor animated Bust*
> *This simple Stone directs Pale Scotia's way*
> *To pour her sorrows o'er her Poets Dust.*

Another milestone for the church had come in 1745 when Bonnie Prince Charlie's prisoners from the Battle of Prestonpans were detained here.

WHITE HORSE CLOSE:

Laurence Ord, merchant and burgess of Edinburgh, built the White Horse Inn and coaching stables here in 1623 and named them after Queen Mary's white palfrey. The stagecoach for Newcastle and London left from the inn. During Bonnie Prince Charlie's occupation of Edinburgh in 1745 his officers whiled away many happy hours supping ale here. The Close was restored in 1965.

SCOTTISH PARLIAMENT:

The new Scottish Parliament building, located on the site of a former brewery, is an award winning design by the late Spanish architect Enric Miralles and was chosen by Scotland's first First Minister, the late Donald Dewar. Mr Dewar like Miralles's vision of a Parliament building sitting on the land and not dominating it.

Scheduled to be up and running in 2004, the building contains the debating chamber, committee rooms, and offices for all 129 MSPs, staff and media representatives.

THE WHITE HORSE INN.

HOLYROOD:

King David I established a house of Augustinian canons at Holyrood in 1128. Like other religious houses it was used by the kings of Scots as guest accommodation. Robert the Bruce and Edward Balliol also held parliaments here. James II was born in the guest house in 1430. In 1501 it was extended by James IV into a royal residence. During 1529-32 the north-west tower was built for King James V as a royal apartment. Charles II had the great sixteenth century tower altered and refurbished (1671-1680) while the rest of the Palace was rebuilt. Oddly enough he never stayed there although his brother, who was later to become King James VII and II, took up residence from time to time. Royal interest then waned until 1822 when George IV made a grand visit to the capital and later Queen Victoria began regular periods of Royal occupation which still continue today. Of the original mediaeval abbey all that remains are the ruined nave of the church and the foundations of its transepts and quire. Stories of Abbey and Palace have of course been covered fully on other pages.

The Vanished Mile

Just outside the castle is Geoffrey (Tailor's) Tartan Weaving Mill, Exhibition and Gift Store. It is a constant bustle of visitors from all over the world but in times past it was the site of the Town's Yard with a fire station, a general depot, and a cistern for water from the Comison Springs.

The cistern, erected in 1851 supplied the wells of the Royal Mile.

In 1681 Bruschi, a Dutchman, first brought water from Comison to the High Street. The City Records state that George Whyte, servant to Bruschi, retained the keys of the water foundations, and that a small pipe was led into the Tolbooth to supply the prisoners with water.

At the time of the second Jacobite Rebellion in 1745 the Highlanders were reported to "have lett owt the town sisteren in Castle hill, and the watter runs down the streats."

In nearby Ramsay Lane Thomas Guthrie (1803-73) established his Ragged School for "city Arabs."

Further down at the Stripping Close, on the south side of Castle Hill, prisoners were obliged to remove their upper garments before being whipped from here to the Netherbow. Three men were whipped as late as July 31, 1822.

This Close contained the printing office of James Donaldson (1751-1830), publisher of the *Edinburgh Advertiser* and founder of Donaldson's Hospital.

THOMAS GUTHRIE, D.D.

The Lawnmarket was The Land Market in Edgar's Plans of the City, 1742 and 1765, the produce of the land, even meat, having been sold here. A later proverb, with another spelling, runs: "As thrang (crowded) as the Lawnmercat." Ainslie's Map of 1780, however, spells the name Lawnmarket.

The Anecdotes and Egotisms of Henry Mackenzie (1745-1831) states: "The Lawn Mercat, the chief quarter for persons of distinction. It used to be a sort of sight to go to a window there and see the ladies walking (which they always did in fair weather) along that street to the tea-parties at five in the afternoon. Dr Monro (1697-1767), one of the founders, it may be said, of the Medical School of Edinburgh, had a house there."

The eighteenth century property of the Baxters or Bakers — Baxter's Close — had to be demolished for the construction of Bank Street.

Robert Burns arrived here from Ayrshire on November 28, 1786, and shared a room with John Richmond, writer's clerk from Mauchline. The landlady charged them one shilling and sixpence each a week (7.5 pence.)

"This month," says Carlyle, "he is a ruined peasant, his wages seven pounds a year, and these gone from him: next month he is in the blaze of rank and beauty, handing down jewelled duchesses to dinner; the cynosure of all eyes."

The citzens of the Castle Hill and Lawnmarket had varied occupations, the Edinburgh Directory during the latter half of the eighteenth century giving the following: money scrivener, inspector of window lights, mantua maker, clothes cleaner, gumflower maker, setter of elegant rooms, fringe manufacturer, extractor, harpsichorn and spinet maker.

It was in the Lawnmarket that the ex-Regent Morton spent the last days of his life, and in his conferences with the clergy protested his innoncence of Darnley's murder. " 'Tis an axe, man, an axe, which falls of itself like a sash window, and never gives the headsman the trouble to wield it," wrote Sir Walter Scott in *The Abbot.*

At the upper end of Old Bank Close Lord President Sir George Lockhart was shot by a disappointed litigant, John Chiesley of Dalry, in 1689. The murderer was hanged with the pistol round his neck. Says Scott in *The Bride of Lammermoor*: "The fate of Chiesley was a sufficient warning to any one who should dare to assume the office of avenger of his own imaginary wrongs."

The Tolbooth Prison, as mentioned briefly in the previous chapter, was situated at the north-west corner of St. Giles. Erected on or before 1561 it was swept away in 1817 when a new jail was built on the Calton Hill.

Victims of the law had their heads stuck in pikes affixed to the north gable wall and and the roof of an annexe formed the scaffold for criminals such as Deacon Brodie.

The following extracts from the Tolbooth register give a flavour of crime and punishment in times past.

1662. June 10. Robert Binning for falsehood: hanged with the false papers about his neck.

July 8. Sir Archibald Johnston of Warrison: treason. Hanged, his head cut off and placed in the Netherbow.

August 13. Robert Reid for murder. His head struck from his body at the Mercat Cross.

December 4. James Ridpath, tinker: to be whipped from Castlehill to Netherbow, burned on the cheek with the town's common mark, and banished the kingdom, for the crime of double adultery.

October 25, 1728. John Gibson: forging a declaration — his lug nailed to the Tron and dismissed.

March 18, 1751. Helen Torrace and Jean Waldie were executed this day for stealing a child, eight or nine years of age, and selling its body to the surgeons for dissection. Alive on Tuesday when carried off and dead on Friday, with an incision in the belly but sewn up again.

The Luckenbooths (i.e. locked booths) were a feature of the High Street until 1817. The passage between the west Luckenbooths and the houses on the north side was some 15 feet wide. "This would be undoubtedly one of the noblest streets in Europe, if an ugly mass of mean buildings, called the Luckenbooths, had not thrust itself, by what accident I know not, into the middle of the way, like Middle-Row in Holborn." (Smollett).

The passage between the Luckenbooths and St Giles was called locally the Krames. "Shopless traffickers first began to nestle there about the year 1550 or 1560, and their successors stuck the spot till 1817, when they were all swept away," says Cockburn.

"In my boyhood their little stands, each enclosed in a tiny room of its own, and during the day all open to the little footpath that ran between the two rows of them, and all glittering with attractions, contained everything fascinating to childhood, but chiefly toys. It was like one of the Arabian Nights bazaars in Baghdad. Throughout the whole year it was an enchantment. Let anyone fancy what it was about the New Year, when every child had got its handsel, and every farthing or every handsel, was spent there. The Krames was the paradise of childhood."

Robert Louis Stevenson wrote: "In one of those little shops plastered like so many swallows' nests among the buttresses of the old Cathedral, that familiar autocraft, King James VI, would gladly share a bottle of wine with George Heriot the Goldsmith."

The Royal Bank was situated at Old Stamp Office Close in High Street from 1727 to 1753. Here too was the famous John Fortune's tavern, a focal point of Edinburgh life in the latter half of the eighteenth century. The Lord High Commissioner to the General Assembly held formal receptions here before proceeding to St Giles. Ladies in court dress formed part of the procession.

The Poker Club, started in 1762, moved to Fortune's. Its members included Adam Ferguson, David Hume, Hugh Blair, Joseph Black and Adam Smith. Political groups met at Fortune's to drink Two-penny, an old Scottish ale, with which "they ate souters' clods, a coarse, lumpish kind of loaf" (Chambers). Scott and Jeffrey, it may be remembered, one day "rushed from George Square" to sup at Fortune's.

It is also said that Flora Macdonald, heroine of the Second Jacobite Rebellion, finished her education here at Miss Henderson's boarding school.

From the cellar at 177 High Street the coach left for South Queensfery, then the Queen's Ferry.

"The lady of the subterranean mansion was then Mrs Macleuchar, a sharp-looking dame, with a pair of spectacles on a very thin nose, who inhabited a 'laigh shop' (that is an area) opening to the High Street by a strait and steep stair, at the bottom of which she sold tape, thread, needles, skeans of worsted, coarse linen cloth, and such feminine gear."

In Carrubers Close, High Street, at the house of Samuel Mitchelson, Writer to the Signet, Matthew Bramble, dined on "singed sheep's head and haggis."

"The first," says Smollett, "put me in mind of the history of Congo, in which I read of negroes' heads sold publicly in the markets. The last, being a mess of minced lights, livers, suet, oat-meal, onions and pepper, enclosed in a sheep's stomach, had a very sudden effect on mine, and the delicate Mrs Tabby changed colour."

On the morning of Sunday November 24, 1861, numbers 99 to 103 High Street "ran together with a hideous uproar and tumbled storey by storey to the ground." Thirty five people were killed.

When the rescuers were at work, a boy called Joseph McIvor who was pinned down by the debris, was heard shouting: "Heave awa' lads, I'm no deid yet."

The keystone of the modern arch bears the boy's head. The civil engineers who reported on the accident gave the cause as "the removal of the large porition of the central wall on the shop floor."

Old Fishmarket Close was the venue, until the dawn of the nineteenth century, of a fishmarket and is described by Cockburn as "a steep, narrow, stinking ravine."

He adds: "The fish were generally thrown out in the street at the head of the Close, whence they were dragged down by dirty boys or dirtier women; and then sold unwashed — for there was not a drop of water in the place — from old, rickety, scaly, wooden tables, exposed to all the rain, dust and filth." Poultry the women disposed of later.

In this close until the start of the twentieth century might have been seen the dwelling of the hangman or doomster. John High, the last recorded hangman, died in 1817. He was also called "the lad in the piot coat", piot meaning magpie. This was because of his livery of black or dark grey being ornamented with silver lace.

There was widespread destruction in the "Great Fire" of 1824 which

HOUSE IN HIGH STREET WITH MEMORIAL WINDOW, "HEAVE AWA, LADS, I'M NO DEID YET!"

RUINS IN PARLIAMENT SQUARE AFTER THE GREAT FIRE.

had its origins in the Old Assembly Close, at the printing premises of Kirkwood and Sons on November 15. Tenements between St Giles and the Tron, with others in the north-eastern corner of the Parliament Close, were quickly alight.

Cockburn reports: "Before morning a range of houses six or seven stories high, with fifteen windows in front and extending back almost to Cowgate — as dense a mass of buildings as was perhaps in the world — was a burnt shell."

The only building in the High Street which escaped destruction — "Salamander Land" — contained the shop of James Donaldson, founder of Donaldson's Hospital. It was demolished in 1847 for the extension of the Police Office.

Despite such hardships our forefathers kept their humour.

Sir Walter Scott, referring to a fire at Tron Church, turned to his companions and said: "Eh, sirs! mony a weary, weary sermond hae I heard beneath that steeple!"

It was also at the Tron that William Erskine, a seventeenth century cleric, exclaimed during prayer: "Lord, have mercy on all fools and idiots, particularly on the magistrates of Edinburgh!"

The town was disorderly in the sixteenth and seventeenth centuries as we can glean from Sir Walter Scott's *The Abbot.*

THE OLD SCOTTISH MINT, HIGH STREET, DEMOLISHED IN 1887.

"Georgfe of Seyton," says Norton to Murray," was crossing the causeway this morning with a score of men at his back, and had a ruffle with my friends of the house of Leslie; they met at the Tron, and were fighting hard, when the provost with his guard of partizans came in thirdsman, and staved them asunder with their halberds, as men part dog and bear."

At World's End Close stood the house of Sir James Stanfield of Newmills, East Lothian, whose murder in 1687 was a mystery connected with the politics of the time of King James VII. The belief that the body of the person murdered bleeds at the touch of the murderer was urged as evidence of guilt at the trial of the son, Philip Stanfield.

Young Stanfield touch'd his father's corpse,
When rose a fearful wail:
For blood gush'd from the winding-sheet,
And every face grew pale.
                                            JAMES MILLER

The Netherbow Port divided Edinburgh from the suburb of Canongate. Bow means 'arch'.

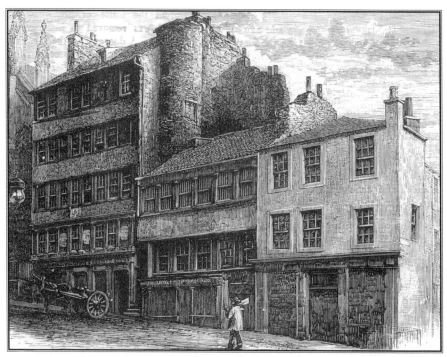

THE EXCISE OFFICE AT THE NETHERBOW. *(After a painting by Alexander A. Inglis.)*

In the '45 Rebellion Prince Charles Edward's followers met with no opposition while entering the Capital by the Netherbow. "Just as the Highlanders reached the gate," writes Chambers, "it was opened by the guard within, in order to let out the hackney coach which had brought back the deputies from Slateford. The coach was returning to the Ramsay stables in the Cowgate. No sooner did the portal open than the Highlanders rushed in and took possession of the gate."

The figure of a Moor with turban and necklace on the front of Morocco Land, Morocco Close, signals a fascinating story. Andrew Gray, ringleader of a disturbance at the home of an unpopular Lord Provost, was arrested and locked up in the Tolbooth. He later escaped and went to sea, rising to high rank in the household of the Emperor of Morocco.

Many years later, in 1645, a Moorish vessel lay at anchor in Leith Roads. The commander, Andrew Gray, inquiring for the provost of his college days, learned that the daughter suffered from plague, and volunteered to cure her. The cure proving satisfactory, he married his patient, setting up house in what has since been called Morocco Land.

Adam Smith, the father of political economics, lived at Panmure Close, Canongate, from 1778 to 1790. His *The Wealth of Nations* argues that every man promotes the interests of his fellows by attending to his own.

When he went to meet Prime Minister Pitt, the PM and other leading dignatories rose from their chairs at Smith entered the room.

"Be seated genetlemen," said the great economist.

But Pitt requested Smith to be seated first "for we are all your scholars."

One Sunday evening the economist was entertaining some friends to supper at Panmure House. Looking ill, he was advised to retire early. Pausing with his hand on the door, he addressed the guests: "I fear I shall never meet you again, but I trust we shall meet in another, a better world." Next Saturday he was dead.

Golfer's Land, Canongate, was built from the winnings of a golf match played over Leith Links whilst the gardens at Moray House were described as the finest in the land.

David Buchanan (1595-1652), who wrote a description of Edinburgh in Latin to accompany Gordon of Rothiemay's Plan of the City, described the residence and gardens as "of such elegance, and cultivated with such diligence, that they easily challenge comparison with the gardens of warmer climates and almost of England itself, and here you may see how much human skill and industry avail in making up for the defects of nature herself."

We end this chapter with a quote from Robert Louis Stevenson on the landmark which marks the end of the Royal Mile.

"Holyrood is a house of many memories," he wrote. "Great people of yore, kings and queens, buffoons and grave ambassadors, played their stately farce for centuries in Holyrood. Wars have been plotted, dancing has lasted deep into the night, murder has been done in its chambers."

GOLFER'S LAND

A tour of the New Town

Our tour of the New Town begins beyond the east end of Princes Street at one of the city's best known landmarks.

CALTON HILL:
For breathtaking views over our northern capital and the Forth drive up to the summit or, if you are feeling more energetic, walk. The National Monument, modelled on the Parthenon, made Calton the Acropolis of Modern Athens. Dedicated to the memory of those who fell in the Napoleonic War, only 12 columns were ever completed, because of financial problems. Nearby is a copy of the monument to Lysicrates in Athens, an observatory designed to reproduce the Temple of the Winds and on the southern side, the finest neo-classical building in Edinburgh, the old Royal High School. The central part of this building — once planned as the seat of Scotland's Assembly and now home of the Crown Office — is a copy of the Theseum, which overlooks the Agora in Athens. By contrast there is the Nelson Monument which is in the form of an inverted telescope. Particularly worth visiting is the Camera Lucida which is housed in the north-east Observatory dome. Opened in 1984 it gives a live view of life around the hill.

THE CALTON HILL, CALTON GAOL, BURYING GROUND, AND MONUMENTS.

OLD CALTON BURYING GROUND:

Across the road, publishers William Blackwood and Archibald Constable and philosopher David Hume are among the famous who are buried here. There is a statue to Abraham Lincoln dedicated to the Scottish-American soldiers who fought in the American Civil War and a Martyrs' Memorial to five early Chartists who were transported because they had agitated for parliamentary reform.

REGISTER HOUSE:

East end of Princes Street. The legal and historical public records of Scotland are kept here, with wills dating from 700 years ago! Robert Adam designed the building and it was completed early in the nineteenth century by Robert Reid.

NEW REGISTER HOUSE:

Next door. The statutory registers of births, deaths and marriages are kept here. The Lord Lyon King of Arms, the nation's arbiter on heraldry and similar subjects, also has his base in the building. Technically the Lyon, through his court, still has the power to behead accused people who have caused offence!

ST ANDREW'S SQUARE:

A church had been planned on the east side to 'match' St George's in Charlotte Square but a member of the influential Dundas family who owned the land built a fine house there instead. Today it is the Royal Bank of Scotland head office. Standing on top of a 130-feet high pillar in the centre of the Square is Henry, first Viscount Melville, who ran Scotland under Pitt. The way he used his wide ranging powers earned him the nickname of 'King Henry IX'.

WAVERLEY MARKET:

Moving back down to Princes Street we come to this shopping complex, situated next to the mighty Balmoral Hotel. The Plaza, with uninterrupted views of historic Edinburgh, has become a communal meeting point. The tourist information centre is situated here.

SCOTT MONUMENT:
The monument to Sir Walter Scott, in the East Gardens, is more than 200 feet high and all you have to do for a commanding view over the city, Forth and surrounding countryside, is climb the 287 steps which lead to an observation area at the top. Designed by George Meikle Kemp this fitting tribute to the fine writer was completed in 1844. There is a statue of Sir Walter under the canopy of the arches and 64 statuettes of characters from his novels and poems are incorporated in the niches. These include Bonnie Prince Charlie, the Lady of the Lake, James Hogg, Robert Burns and Meg Merrilees.

ROYAL SCOTTISH ACADEMY (1826)
and the
NATIONAL GALLERY OF SCOTLAND (1859):
Both are designed on the lines of the Grecian buildings on Calton Hill and the old Royal High School. The R.S.A., founded to promote the fine arts in Scotland such as painting, sculpture and architecture, holds an annual exhibition between April and August. From late April to early August the Academy presents an exhibition of the work of its elected members and other contemporary artists. The National Gallery's collection is largely given over to the works of Continental and English masters from the fourteenth century to Cezanne although there is of course a significant section devoted to Scottish artists.

THE ROYAL INSTITUTION, NOW THE ROYAL SCOTTISH ACADEMY, 1880.

FLORAL CLOCK:
In West Princes Street Gardens the Floral Clock, incorporating some 24,000 plants and flowers, usually has a topical design to mark a particular gathering or event which is taking place. It's the oldest floral clock in the world and has a big hand weighing 80 pounds and one which is 30 pounds lighter. A cuckoo pops out to mark the quarter hour.

ROYAL SCOTS MONUMENT:
Situated just down from the Floral Clock and dedicated in 1952 to the British Army's oldest regiment of the line. Here also can be seen the Scottish American War Memorial, which was put up by Americans of Scots descent as a tribute to the courage shown by men from the old country in the First World War, and the Royal Scots Greys Monument, erected in memory of those who fell in the South African war at the turn of the twentieth century. It depicts a rider and horse, one third larger than life size, mounted on a rock base. The centrepiece of the Scottish American Memorial shows a young soldier gazing towards the castle.

ST CUTHBERT'S CHURCH:
This West End church is the second oldest religious institution in Edinburgh. The present building dates from 1892 and doesn't contain anything of the original mediaeval structure. Among the worthies buried in the churchyard are Alexander Napier of Merchistoun, inventor of logarithms, and the author Thomas De Quincey. A point of interest is a stone built tower with blocked up windows which stands in the south west corner of the graveyard. It is a watch tower built in 1827 so that bereaved relatives could protect their loved ones from the dreaded body-snatchers who robbed graves for doctors.

ST JOHN'S EPISCOPAL CHURCH:
Situated at the corner of Lothian Road and Princes Street. The people interred in its cemetery include James Donaldson, the founder of Donaldson's School for the Deaf, and the painter Sir Henry Raeburn.

EDINBURGH FROM THE SOUTH, 1650.

THE GEORGIAN HOUSE:

7 Charlotte Square. The ground floor, first floor and basement were converted by the National Trust for Scotland to show living conditions and styles as they were when the house was first occupied in 1796. The newly built residence was bought in that year by the 18th chief of Clan Lamont for the princely sum of £1,800! An idea of changing property values in those far off times can be gleaned from records which show that the house was sold nineteen years later for £3,000. Today the top two floors form the official residence of the Moderator of the General Assembly of the Church of Scotland. The Trust had the happy idea of opening the period showhouse in 1973. As the official guide book states: "Although the New Town of Edinburgh was one of the finest examples of 18th century town planning and people could enjoy the splendid squares, crescents and streets of houses externally, there was no opportunity of seeing the inside of a house unless one was visiting one's dentist or lawyer, and even then one's mind would undoubtedly be occupied with other matters". Furnishings are mainly from the 1790-1810 era. The tour of the house takes in Entrance Hall, Inner Hall, Dining Room, Bed Chamber, Drawing Room, Parlour, Basement, Kitchen, Wine Cellar, and The China Closet.

ASSEMBLY ROOMS:
George Street. This has been a meeting place for Edinburgh folk since the eighteenth century. There are a suite of rooms which provide seating ranging between 150 to 1,200. The impressive Assembly Room has great crystal chandeliers and can be used as a ballroom, for banqueting or conferences. In 1827 the anonymous writer of the Waverley novels was revealed at the Assembly Rooms as Sir Walter Scott.

SCOTTISH NATIONAL PORTRAIT GALLERY
and the
NATIONAL MUSEUM OF ANTIQUITIES:
Both situated at the east end of Queen Street. Portraits in the Gallery are of many famous Scots and date from the mid-sixteenth century. The museum contains an invaluable collection representing the history and everyday life of Scotland from the Stone Age. These institutions were originally launched with a £30,000 donation from an Edinburgh citizen who wished to remain anonymous. In later years he was revealed as John Findlay, proprietor of *The Scotsman* — the Scottish broadsheet newspaper which is now produced from offices at Holyrood Road. The red sandstone building which houses these two fine institutions was designed by Sir Rowand Anderson at the end of the nineteenth century and has a resemblance to the Doge's Palace in Venice.

20 facts about the New Town

1. In 1766 Edinburgh magistrates bought the land required to build the first new town. A competition was announced for its layout. The winner was James Craig, a 23-year-old architect. On June 3 of that year he was awarded a gold medal and freedom of the City for his efforts.

2. Craig's layout was a gridiron designed as a formal symmetrical whole. Two churches were planned for each end although, as is explained elsewhere, only the one in Charlotte Square was built.

3. The design was intended to symbolise the equal partnership of Scotland and England under the Crown.

4. Craig died in poverty in 1796. He was buried in Greyfriars Churchyard.

5. There were no shops in the main streets until early in the nineteenth century when a few select establishments began to appear on the ground floors of houses.

6. Robert Adam was commissioned by the town council in 1791 to provide a plan and complete elevations for Charlotte Square. This followed complaints about the haphazard development of the new town. Work started in the following year and all the houses were completed in Craigleith stone.

7. This square was once known as the Harley Street of Edinburgh because so many doctors lived there — among them Professor Lister, the pioneer in antiseptic surgery. He stayed at number 9 from 1870 to 1877.

8. A second new town to the north of Craig's layout was planned with a greater emphasis on architectural unity from the start. This takes in the Gloucester Place, Great King Street and Drummond Place areas.

9. In 1822, a third development began on the Earl of Moray's estate. People who bought land here undertook to maintain the highest quality and styles. Developments followed designs drawn up by James Gillepsie and by 1827 nearly all of the building plots had been disposed of as demand was very brisk. The Great Stuart Street, Randolph Crescent, Ainslie Place and Moray Place areas flourished as a result.

10. Nine years earlier Gillepsie had produced his master plan for the West End but development was slow because of the large number of different feudal superiors and architects involved. In due course it was finished and extended with Victorian terraces. Their elaborate classical facades never forgot the dignity of the Georgian tradition.

11. Most of the area from Melville Street to Coates Crescent was designed by Robert Brown in 1813. Stafford Street was designed in 1819 and Alva Street in 1823.

12. Melville Street dates from 1855. St. Mary's Cathedral at the end of the street was designed by Sir George Gilbert Scott in 1879. Rutland Square was planned in 1819 and building began 11 years later.

13. In times past the attractions of the new town's squares and terraces were obvious when viewed against the cramped living conditions of the old town tenements. The open outlook and self contained living accommodation enticed the likes of lawyers and merchants away from the foul smelling 'communal' houses of the Royal Mile where there was not even running water.

14. Servants were employed to keep the new houses clean and tidy. Manservants earned £10 a year; maidservants half that amount

15. Entertaining at home as opposed to spending one's evenings in the taverns became fashionable. Large dinner parties were followed by chat, cards and dancing. There were nights out at the ball in the Assembly Rooms or to the Theatre Royal. Those who liked the outdoor life could golf over Bruntsfield Links, watch the horses race at Leith, bathe in the sea at Trinity and, in deep winter, skate over Duddingston Loch.

16. George Drummond, who was Lord Provost of Edinburgh for six terms of office, had translated the 50-year-old dream of building a new town into a reality. The Nor Loch at the base of the Castle (Princes Street Gardens today) was drained and the North Bridge constructed over its valley to give easier access to the proposed new community and port of Leith. Other Scottish towns contributed money for the building of a new Exchange to promote trade.

17. In 1824, 79 oil lamps which lit Princes Street were replaced with 53 gas lanterns. Within six years most of the houses were gas lit. The electric light came to prominence in April, 1895, when a new £120,000 system was switched on.

18. In 1876 Princes Street Gardens were opened to the public. Smoking was banned although towards the end of the century, as attitudes became more relaxed, this rule was dropped.

19. The sedan chair and carriages were popular forms of transport but in 1898 there was great cheering and much excitement when the first motor bus ran from the GPO to Haymarket.

20. Two centuries of exposure to the elements have obviously taken their toll on new town buildings and since 1972 millions of pounds have been spent on conservation work. This has included the replacement of missing features such as balustrades, glazing bars and cast ironwork. Today the restorations still go on to ensure that our descendants 200 years from now will be able to enjoy the delights of the New Town.

ADAM'S DESIGN FOR ST. GEORGE'S CHURCH, CHARLOTTE SQUARE.

Other Scottish bestsellers from Lang Syne

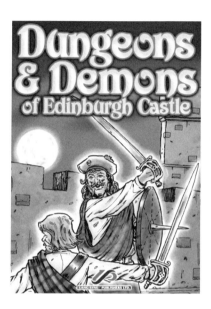

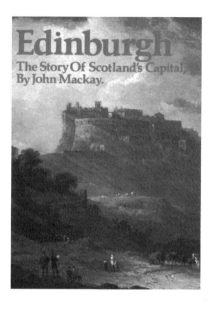

Dungeons & Demons of Edinburgh Castle

If the stones of Edinburgh Castle could talk, what strange tales they would tell: of murder and torture, of magic and witchcraft, of intrigues and kidnappings, of sieges and sabotage. This book is a must for anyone fascinated by the dark and daring deeds of yesteryear.

ISBN 1-85217-149-9 £2.99

Edinburgh: The Story of Scotland's Capital

John Mackay's light-hearted history tells the story of Edinburgh from the earliest times – and consequently also mirrors the development of Scotland as a nation. Discover how the shaping of Edinburgh was the making of Scotland.

ISBN 1-852170-06-9 £3.95

Lang**Syne**

PUBLISHING

WRITING *to* REMEMBER

Other Scottish bestsellers from Lang Syne

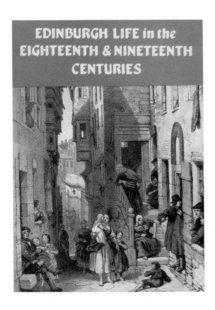

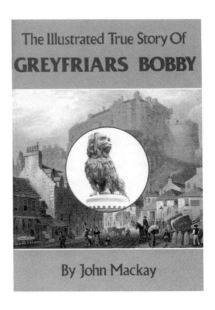

Edinburgh Life in the Eighteenth and Nineteenth Centuries

Two books in one. Letters written from Edinburgh in 1775 by an English army officer describing life and times in the city and Henry Grey Graham's account of the teeming wynds and taverns. The book on the 19th century is told in a year by year diary of famous events.
ISBN 1-852170-03-4 £5.99

Greyfriars Bobby

The remarkable story of the little dog who kept watch over his master's grave for 14 years. This account by John Mackay is one of the best detailing, with the aid of copious illustrations, the little Skye terrier's devotion to his master, Edinburgh policeman John Gray.
ISBN 0-946264-45-7 £3.95

LangSyne
PUBLISHING
WRITING *to* REMEMBER

Other Scottish bestsellers from Lang Syne

Massacre of Glencoe

John Buchan, author of *The Thirty-Nine Steps*, tells the true story of one of the most shameful and disgraceful acts of betrayal in Scotland's long and turbulent history.

ISBN 1-85217-164-2 £5.99

Strange Tales of Old Edinburgh

Witches, ghosts, crimes of passion, taverns with many a tale to tell – from Corstorphine to Morningside, Cramond to Gilmerton and Joppa to Juniper Green – Ian Ansdell unlocks the secrets of dark deeds and foul play.

ISBN 0-946264-53-8   £3.95

Lang**Syne**

PUBLISHING

WRITING *to* REMEMBER

Other Scottish bestsellers from Lang Syne

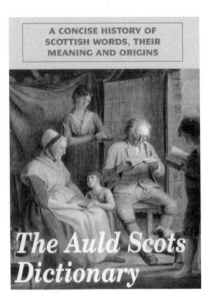

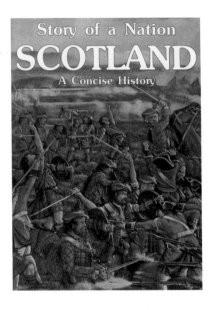

Auld Scots Dictionary

A concise history of Scottish words, their meanings and origins. Discover where those marvellous old Scots words like drookit, glaikit, gawkie, flunkey, muckle, pernickitie, cannie, carfuffle, whitter and dour came from.
ISBN 1-85217-001-8   £10.95

Story of a Nation

One of the most authoritative histories of Scotland, telling our nation's story in a bright, concise style. The text includes illustrations, maps, a list of events, of sovereigns and genealogical tables, and is fully indexed.
ISBN 1-85217-170-7   £10.95

Lang**Syne**
PUBLISHING
WRITING *to* REMEMBER